THEY BECAME
WHAT
THEY BEHELD

THEY BECAME WHAT THEY BEHELD

**WRITTEN BY
EDMUND CARPENTER
PHOTOGRAPHED BY
KEN HEYMAN**

AN OUTERBRIDGE & DIENSTFREY / BALLANTINE BOOK

Outerbridge & Dienstfrey, Distributed by E. P. Dutton

Ballantine Books, Inc., An INTEXT Publisher, New York

The text owes much to Marshall McLuhan who, in
fact, co-authored portions of an earlier version. We are
indebted to the authors quoted and to their publishers,
and to *Harper's Bazaar* in which some portions of the
material appeared.

The Tribal Man who walks through these pages
is composed, like the Bride of Frankenstein, of bits
& pieces from many sources. He cannot be found
in any nearby jungle or tundra or city, but lives in a more
remote land, in company with the savages of
Rousseau & Diderot.

Library of Congress number 73-129502
First published in the United States of America in 1970
Copyright © 1970 by Edmund Carpenter and Ken Heyman
All rights reserved, including the right of
reproduction in whole or in part in any form.

Design: Hess and/or Antupit

Outerbridge & Dienstfrey
200 West 72 Street, New York 10023

Ballantine Books, Inc.
101 Fifth Avenue
New York, N. Y. 10003

FOREWORD

I recently came across the following rules of communication, posted in a School of Journalism:

1. Know your audience and address yourself directly to it.
2. Know what you want to say and say it clearly and fully.
3. Reach the maximum audience by utilizing existing channels.

Whatever sense this may have made in a world of print, it makes no sense today. In fact, the reverse of each rule applies.

If you address yourself to an audience, you accept at the outset the basic premises that unite the audience. You put on the audience, repeating clichés familiar to it. But artists don't address themselves to audiences; they create audiences. The artist talks to himself out loud. If what he has to say is significant, others hear & are affected.

The trouble with knowing what to say and saying it clearly & fully, is that clear speaking is generally obsolete thinking. Clear statement is like an art object: it is the afterlife of the process which called it into being. The process itself is the significant step and, especially at the beginning, is often incomplete & uncertain. Columbus's maps were vague & sketchy, but showed the right continent.

The problem with full statement is that it doesn't involve: it leaves no room for participation; it's addressed to consumer, not co-producer. Allan Kaprow posted a few small posters about Berkeley: ''SUPPOSE you were interested in designing a primer, in mixed media, etc. . . . Allan Kaprow will be in Berkeley in July & August.'' No phone, address, dates, terms. He found, however, that those who wanted to work with him, and those he wanted to work with, located him without difficulty.

Reaching the maximum audience may be the last thing one wants to achieve. George Segal says, ''I don't give myself to everybody. I give myself very intensely to my work, my wife, my kids, my few friends. I can't begin to give myself indiscriminately to all. It's the only thing that makes me pause about, say,

Ginsberg's preachings of universal love or even California ideas about Esalen and touching.''

Utilizing existing channels can wipe out a statement. There is a widely accepted misconception that media merely serve as neutral packages for the dissemination of raw facts. Photographers once thought that by getting their photographs published in *Life,* they would thereby reach large audiences. Gradually they discovered that the only message that came through was *Life* magazine itself and that their pictures had become but bits & pieces of that message. Unwittingly they contributed to a message far removed from the one they intended.

The same thing occurs on TV guest shows. Guests accept invitations to appear on programs in the hopes their messages will reach new & wider audiences, but even when they are treated in a friendly manner, they generally come away with a sense of failure. Somehow the message transmitted is far removed from the message intended. The original message has been declassified by an alien medium. ''Oh, what a blow that phantom gave me!'' cries Don Quixote.

The young today shun the hardware of the past. Marx thought the big question was: Who owns the presses? Software makes hardware obsolete, an encumbrance, creating a false sense of power & security. The young package their messages in media that fit their messages, that is, they create new media to fit their messages. In so doing, they create their own audiences. Some of these audiences may be very small at the beginning. In Houston I met film makers producing films for audiences of no more than six. The point was that they would reach the right people in the right way with the right message.

It is one of the curiosities of a new medium, a new format, that at the moment it first appears, it's never valued, but it is believed. What it offers, I believe, is a sudden insight, an unexpected glimpse into a reality that, at most, was merely suspected but never before seen with such clarity.

Like guerillas, the young are in a favored position; they don't need or want the hardware & audiences of yesterday.

DISLOCATIONS

Only connect; the rest is silence.

AS IT WAS IN THE BEGINNING. IS NOW AND EVER SHALL BE. WORLD WITHOUT END.

"Contemporary art was born out of the urge for elemental expression. The artist plunged into the depths of human experience. A real inner affinity suddenly appeared between the longings of the man of today and the longings of primeval man, crystallized in signs and symbols on the cavern walls." *S. Giedion*

This notebook of juxtaposed images & explorations is organized around correspondences between certain preliterate & postliterate experiences. To convey the essence of these experiences to a contemporary audience, in the idiom of our day, I felt it necessary to find literary expressions consonant with the experiences themselves. The rhythms practiced here are heightened, concentrated & frequently more violent than those found in more conventional texts. They belong to the world of icon & music, graffiti & cartoon, and lie closer, I believe, to the original experiences.

These rhythms include interval (with abrupt interface) & repeat/repeat of cliché (with slight variation), a technique made familiar by Andy Warhol and common to much tribal art.

In the 1960's, people spoke of "dropping out."
No more. Dropping out, like suicide, involved a choice.
Now there's no choice: the system itself has dropped
out.

Human evolution began in South Africa, not when
apes descended from trees, but when the trees
themselves disappeared & arboreal skills became
obsolete.

Electronic media created a new environment,
rendering obsolete the patterns by which literate man
codified reality. Suddenly, all information — freed from
classifications which had long bound it — became
raw data, available to everyone simultaneously via
electronic media.

Out of this vastly confusing wealth, each of us is
forced to create his own environment — that is,
program his own psychic & sensory life. To this end
we turn to the arts, for only artists, and maybe
criminals, create their own lives.

"To live outside the law you must be honest."
Bob Dylan

"I'll go to jail before I'll break the law." *Bumper
sticker*

THE NAME IS THE NUMB

When a cop writes down your name, he takes you over.

As long as information is classified — in content, medium, audience—it's restricted & controlled. But changing any one of these three declassifies it. And the moment it's declassified, all its resources become available to everyone & can be used for new ends. At this point, communication becomes possible.

By "communication" I mean redistribution of knowledge, not simply between knower & not-knower, but ultimately within the intelligence itself.

If we accept the idea that communication automatically excludes the familiar & predictable, then most so-called communication media are grossly mislabeled. Everything in *Reader's Digest* is either familiar or predictable to all its readers. That's why they subscribe. Last month's issue is identical with this month's issue. If you've seen them all, you've seen one. What you've seen is a particular format, and once having experienced that, you know it. Repeating it merely establishes it as cliché. It's like an Anglican sermon that confirms you in all previous convictions. Such convictions are public, shared alike by all subscribers. Publishing them means "putting on the audience." It re-presents that audience to itself.

Newspapers are mirrors; a few even call themselves that. They reflect their readers. Their repeat/repeat of cliché is closer to incantation than to communication.

Some years ago I came across a book entitled *Plots that Sell to Top-paying Magazines* which outlined the storylines each national magazine accepted.

Henry Miller tells how, in hard times, he looked at back issues of magazines, rewrote their stories & submitted these to the editors, who accepted them, of course.

Most journals, newspapers, TV shows, etc., merely repeat clichés & the real clichés they repeat are their own formats. As clichés, they become environmental & hence unseen.

Cyril Connolly once complained that several years after he stopped publishing *Horizons,* contributors were still submitting articles.

In the novel *Jean Barois,* the founder & editor of a small but once-influential magazine continues to publish long after his magazine has had any effects. Finally he runs an experiment: for three months he fails to send copies to twenty charter subscribers though their subscriptions are paid up. Not one of them notices.

About fifteen years ago, someone checked the circulation of a well-known university quarterly. He found that, of its 700-odd subscribers, less than thirty-five were noninstitutional, and most of these were elderly alumni or department heads. He arranged to have several libraries place current & back issues on reserve. No one checked them out. Year after year, articles were typed, read, edited, set in type, proofread, printed, mailed, cataloged, even bound, but . . .

When *Life* was young, it succeeded in communicating a new format, a new way of perceiving & classifying experience. It created its own audience by changing people. But in so doing, it fused imperceptibly with the very environment it helped create. Its format, once startling, became an unseen cliche.

Both *Colliers* & *Saturday Evening Post* died at the peak of their circulations. *Life* & *Time* have never had larger circulations, yet both are in financial difficulty. Advertisers feel that products advertised in them tend to disappear into that unseen environment where perception & awareness are muted.

No environment is perceptible because it saturates the whole field of attention. One can perceive it only after alienation—after some degree of alienation. I can swallow the saliva in my mouth because it's "me," but I can't swallow it if I put it first in a glass.

So long as I transact with my environment—my ecological whole—I can't perceive it; it doesn't even environ me. It's an extension of me. And I can't smell myself.

DECLASSIFICATION

When you declassify anything, you make it available for new classification, that is, for the production & distribution of new knowledge. "Congestion," says McLuhan, "is the indispensable prelude to getting your hand in the other guy's pocket."

As McLuhan points out, every breakdown is a potential breakthrough. The 1929 crash revealed the economic structure to the entire community. The breakdown of segregation revealed the nature of racism. The generation gap revealed the nature of identity.

OBSOLESCENCE

Every time you put a new technology around a society, the old technology becomes a junkyard. But from junkyards come new art. New art can be made by retrieving & reshaping junk.

Yeats, after searching widely for the components of new art, finally found them, he tells us, in the "foul rag and bone shop of the heart."

"One touch of nature makes the whole world kin,
That all with one consent praise new-born gauds,
Though they are made and moulded of things past,
And give to dust that is a little gilt
More laud than gilt o'erdusted."
Troilus and Cressida, III, iii

Picasso assembled his famous Bull's Head sculpture from parts of a wrecked bicycle: "Out of the handle bars and the bicycle seat I made a bull's head which everybody recognized as a bull's head. Thus.a metamorphosis was completed and now I would like to see another metamorphosis take place in the opposite direction. Suppose my bull's head is thrown [back] on the scrap heap. Perhaps some day a fellow will come along and say: 'Why there's something that would come in very handy for the handlebars of my bicycle. . . .' "

In a trash heap you can see true forms because everything is declassified. It's a "found art" world. A bright, new, chrome Ford can be driven only in certain areas, in certain ways, for certain purposes. But as junk, it's declassified and all its potentials, hitherto largely concealed by specialization, become accessible to artists. Any junkyard is potentially an alchemist's kitchen, a poet's scrapbook. *The Golden Bough,* all junk, became a source book for poets & writers.

What goes into an attic as useless may be brought back out as art. Trash & Treasures, a sign on a New York shop, serves to remind us that these two aren't necessarily opposites.

Every age has its great poem & that poem is the culture's junkyard: *The Iliad, The Waste Land.*

The anthropologist is the "old rag & bone man" of the world, a title, in fact, conferred by Naskapi Indians on the great ethnologist Frank Speck. Rubbing faces between two worlds in continuous parallel releases archetypes.

Cliche is whatever is in use & whatever is in use is environmental, hence largely invisible. The moment a new cliché arises to surround it, the old cliche becomes useless, hence very visible. Art is often shaped out of the useless archetypes coming from junkyards: they are obsolete clichés, rear-view mirrors.

The wealth & resources of any language or technology become accessible to artists when that language or technology is rendered obsolete by a new form. The Renaissance used Latin & the Classics as art sources. Americans have long treated the whole of Europe & Asia as collectors' junkyards.

Electronic media have turned the entire globe into a midden. Artists are now busy transforming all our yesterdays into now. The whole world has become a happening.

We might liken it to disarmament & demobilization of an army. Materials & talents, hitherto restricted to specific tasks, can now be applied in vastly expanded ways.

THE VISIBLE PAST

The old environment is easier to perceive than the present environment because no one is really involved in it.

When industrialization blackened Leeds & Manchester, creating "this dark, Satanic land," Lake Poets went in search of pastorial pleasures and Wordsworth sang of childhood joys. Classicism served as counterpoint to Renaissance technology; Romanticism to mechanization; Tribalism to electrification. Constructed as countersituations, they provided a means of direct attention. Like utopias, they served as antienvironments enabling one to perceive with detachment & clarity.

Henry Ford used profits from his Rouge River assembly plant to create Dearborn Village filled with churns, spinning wheels & other remnants of cottage handicraft.

Each new development makes an art form of the past. Rome was oriented toward Greece. The Renaissance was oriented toward Rome. American industrialists collected Renaissance paintings. The Museum of Modern Art is really a period piece.

In its initial stages, every new medium takes as its content the medium it has just rendered obsolete: scribes recorded oral legends; printers set in type old manuscripts; Hollywood filmed books; radio broadcast concerts & vaudeville; TV showed old movies; magnetic tape was used to copy LP records.

"Content" in art is often no more than obsolete art serving as facade for new art or new technology. The content of much Renaissance art was the Bible, but its effects derived primarily from single perspective, or private point of view, which was the visual counterpart of the notion of individualism. Both were by-products of writing & the new technology of print.

Each new environment makes the old one visible: what is psychic becomes explicit only after it becomes obsolete. The present environment is never seen. We respect its laws without being conscious of them. We are conscious only of the obsolete & we value it because it appears manageable, subject to conscious control. This makes it splendidly attractive.

The history of European art is a succession of schools & styles replacing one another as new technologies created new ways of perceiving & being, and new ways of perceiving & being created new technologies. Perceptual modes became visible as soon as they became obsolete. They served as the content of each new environment.

I doubt if the same principle operates nearly so clearly in tribal societies. Such societies are highly stable, at least in comparison to Western ones, and among them the dichotomy between the invisible present & the visible past seems far less clear.

"The true mystery of the world is the visible, not the invisible." *Wilde*

THE ISLANDER

"We don't know who discovered water, but we're certain it wasn't a fish." *John Culkin*

It's the outsider who sees the environment. The islander sees the outline of the distant mainland. When he goes ashore, he commands, for he alone sees form & process.

Yeats, Joyce, Shaw, from Ireland; Eliot, from Missouri; Pound, from Idaho, were the innovators of twentieth century English. Beaverbrook, from the Maritimes; Luce. from a missionary family in China; Thomson, from the Ontario bush, became the giants of twentieth century publishing. Detachment & perspective permit pattern recognition.

"In the histories of most peoples, there occur long lapses during which they lie creatively fallow. Western European man was late by a millenium or so in adding anything to ancient culture; the Jews between the Despersion and their emergence from the ghettos did nothing that a historian of art and thought could not cover in a long footnote. When they reentered the world, the Jews, as though seeing for the first time the structure to whose piecemeal growth they had contributed almost nothing, produced within a century a series of epic innovators—Karl Marx, Sigmund Freud, Albert Einstein—and scores of hardly less original (Kafka, for example). The reemergence of the Islamic peoples, when complete, may give us the same kind of constellation." *A. J. Liebling*

WIDE-EYED WONDER OF THE CHILD

All discovery is accident or error Ignorance & inadequacies leave openings for errors & therefore discoveries. No experts need apply.

The phrase "organized ignorance" seems to have arisen during World War II, when Operations Research people put biologists & psychologists to work on weapons problems that would ordinarily have fallen to the lot of engineers & physicists. The former group had all the fresh, wide-eyed wonder of children. They swarmed all over each problem instead of beaming a ray of specialized knowledge at it. If you beam knowledge at a subject, you find it quite opaque; if you organize your ignorance, tacking the situation as an overall project, probing all aspects at the same time, you find unexpected aperatures, vistas, breakthroughs. Thus the chemist Mendeleev, to discover the missing link in the element chart, did not simply use available knowledge. Instead, he asked: what must be the characteristics of the rest, if those we do know are to make sense among themselves?

Organized ignorance can be a great asset when approaching the unfamiliar.

It was this approach of nonpreconception that enabled the film maker Robert Flaherty to discover forms hidden from conventional view. Non-preconception is the precondition to discovery, because it's a state of mind. When you do not preconceive, then you go about finding out. There is nothing else you can do. You begin to explore.

"All art," said Flaherty, "is a kind of exploring. To discover and reveal is the way every artist sets about his business."

Flaherty didn't begin with a script or "point of view," but let the camera see everything, avid as a child, filled with childlike wonder. He did more: he called out forms that the camera found hidden there, for it requires a creative human act before the world explored becomes a world revealed.

"All truths lie waiting in all things," wrote Whitman. "They unfold themselves more fragrant than . . . roses from living buds, whenever you fetch the spring sunshine moistened with summer rain. But it must be in yourself. It shall come from your soul. It shall be love."

DISCOVERING

"Truth will not stand or stay or keep; . . . it is either new or not at all." *Norman O. Brown*

The young were attracted to Eugene McCarthy when he spoke out; they were turned off by Robert Kennedy's hesitancy.

Robert Watts, in creating Happenings, found that Happenings announced far in advance were ignored or forgotten. Participants were drawn to them when they saw them *about* to happen, even beginning to happen.

The young are indifferent to old truths, which are dead, or the possession of others. And they are indifferent to future truths, which are too remote for identity. For them, the act of discovering is primary & personal. It's that moment of inception: quivering with life & uncertainty, vital, subjective. To them, truth = discovering.

"A new form always seems to be more or less an absence of any form at all, since it is unconsciously judged by reference to consecrated forms."— *Robbe-Grillet*

Recognition of any new form is greatly delayed by idle responses of mere like or dislike, satisfaction or alarm. These postures delay any understanding of the real character & function of any new form.

Specialists don't welcome discovery: they welcome only new proofs of what they already know. Discovery is unrepeatable. All specialists understand that discoveries are fatal to the stockpile of their unclassified data. Discovery makes the field of the specialist obsolete.

"Though we all know, we often forget, that the existence of America was one of the greatest disappointments in the history of Europe. Plans laid and hardships borne in the hope of reaching Cathay, merely ushered in a period during which we became to America what the Huns had been to us." *C. S. Lewis*

THE SMELL OF NEWNESS

"Children shudder at the smell of newness as a dog does when it scents a hare. . . ." *Isaac Babel*

Lionel Trilling tells how Robert Warshow gave a toy, outgrown by his own son, to Trilling's son:

"It was a magnificent fortress, with battlements and a drawbridge and a considerable complement of rather splendid lead soldiers. Everything was in excellent condition, nothing was lacking to make it a fine present." But Warshow had added a brand-new box of grenadiers. "He explained, when we protested this extravagance, that to a boy it would not have been a present unless there was something new—it would have been a thing given but not a present."

"The gardener in England," writes Margaret Mead, "lives upon newness and difference. One flower or a border blooms earlier or later, and another is not there at all. The light catches on a new clump of larkspur, and the garden is new made. And in New Guinea the dusty old woven basketry masks are hauled out of the attic of the men's houses, and made new again with fresh feathers and bright flowers arranged in new combinations, with small, graceful, painted birds made of cordlike wood and poised lightly on swaying reed stems."

The magician's paraphernalia are always freshly painted. He creates: what he pulls from a hat is new—just now called into being.

IGNORING OLD AUDIENCE, CREATING NEW

Today's revolutionary movement began with an inspired use of the newly invented LP record. Black humorists, denied access to mass radio audiences, created LP audiences. Though some of these were large, they possessed a sense of intimacy, even conspiracy, totally lacking in radio audiences. When Mort Sahl & others later turned to TV, Black Humor died. Sahl attributed this to political changes, but I wonder if another factor wasn't involved: restricting information makes it highly explosive, while widely disseminating information neutralizes its effects.

DECLASSIFYING THE AUDIENCE

The SDS regularly declassifies university files and the FBI regularly declassifies SDS meetings. Recently the SDS rifled Harvard's files and published a letter from the Dean to the President, written just after the faculty overwhelmingly voted to recommend that the administration deprive the ROTC of course credits & professional standing for those who taught it. The Dean's letter confidentially and informally advised the President that "I disagree with many of the particulars, and virtually all of the spirit of the resolution passed by my own Faculty," and suggested four methods of circumventing the expressed will of his faculty in this matter. Publication of this letter created a whole new ball game.

Last year, *Who's Who in the CIA,* published in East Berlin, listed American agents by name, age, address, specialty, etc. Obviously the Communists know a lot about the CIA. Only Americans are kept ignorant, at least officially. But recently the *Los Angeles Free Press* published sections from this register, which was originally compiled with the aid of Soviet Intelligence!

When Philby went over to the Russians, he declassified all he knew of Allied Intelligence by publishing it in America. Fulbright sought to declassify the Tonkin Inlet incident by releasing it at home. There was no point

in releasing it to Communists since they already knew every detail.

An explosive that is tightly encased has far greater power than one openly exposed. This is often true of information, at least in terms of audience. When classified information is diffused, it's *de-fused*.

This Magazine is About Schools publishes items taken from school bulletin boards, intrafaculty memos, etc., most beyond parody. Fifteen years ago *Explorations* reprinted items lifted from the files of broadcasters & publishers, *e.g.,* Proctor & Gamble's rules on TV censorship, *Life* editor's instructions on creating news, etc. Printing this may have been illegal, but no action was ever brought. By declassifying the audience, the power of restricted information is neutralized and those who once sought to control it are rendered impotent & clownish.

Recently on one California campus, the Chancellor charged two senior faculty with misconduct during a demonstration. Evidence offered in support of one of the charges, all of which were labeled confidential, included testimony of a clerk who had searched wastepaper baskets. The defendants met this problem openly: they printed & widely disseminated the charges. They went further: they enlarged the paragraph on wastepaper snooping into posters which they posted on trees about the campus. Almost immediately the problem ceased to exist, having been publicly purged. In the end, everyone acted as if the whole event had never really happened.

One is reminded of Nixon purging himself on TV by converting a secret donation into public drama before a mass audience.

In Prague, the Czechs reprinted—without change or comment—articles from *Pravda* dealing with the Russian takeover. Czechs read these as high comedy. Russian occupation leaders had to ask *Pravda* to lay off the nonsense.

In other words, by declassifying information & making it available to those to whom it had hitherto been denied, an opposite effect was achieved.

HUMOR AS DECLASSIFIER

One of Will Roger's funniest acts was simply to read the daily newspaper aloud in a night club. Audiences were convulsed. Mort Sahl's only prop was a copy of the *Los Angeles Times.* When Frank Sinatra played the tape of Nixon's 1962 Farewell Speech in a night club, the combination of speech & laughter was so funny, it was released as an LP record.

Today the Yippies, instead of putting politics into the night club, put the night club into politics. When Jerry Rubin, dressed as Santa Claus with a plastic burp gun, appeared before the House Un-American Activities Committee, the comic nature of this Committee was suddenly exposed. In less than an hour, the Committee lost its identity. It tried to solve this by renaming itself.

TRANSLATION

One of the most effective means of declassification is translation, for language is itself a classificatory system.

When you translate from one medium to another, you declassify. When you print an oral tradition, show a movie on TV, film Greek drama, or put a classroom lecture on TV, you declassify both content & medium, and expose both to scrutiny.

Recently in Houston an artist announced a Happening, complete with lights, sound, drama. After the audience had assembled, he wheeled a TV set on stage, plugged it in, turned it on & left. The audience watched TV with growing uneasiness and, for many, growing awareness.

ENTHRONING A NEW MEDIUM, DETHRONING AN OLD

The appearance of any new medium leads to a shift in media ratios, recasting the roles of all older media. Every culture has a primary medium for the classification of that culture's basic clichés. When a new medium replaces it, the old one is freed and takes up its role as a declassifier. The coming of writing enabled one to say what could not be written, and with the coming of print, one could write what couldn't be printed. The coming of films freed the stage for new & bolder drama, just as the appearance of TV freed films.

The older medium is thus free to play a subversive role, much favored by artists but deplored by those grown accustomed to speak with the voice of authority. The *New York Times* & *Life* magazine now find themselves uneasy in their role as critic. Before TV, both spoke in the name of the Establishment. Emmett Hughes, editor of *Life,* was Eisenhower's chief speech writer; his editorials & Presidential speeches were identical. The *New York Times* knew of Kennedy's plan to build up forces in Vietnam, but chose, in the interests of national security, "to minimize its coverage of this crucial event." James Reston knew of the U-2 flights fourteen months before the story broke. In the past, the White House felt free to confide to the Establishment press. No more. *Life* now exposes corruption in government, and the *New York Times* no longer suppresses news on request from the White House. The White House is reported to share classified information now only with TV networks. Print has joined the declassifiers. The press has gone underground.

MATING MEDIA

Mating two media can simultaneously declassify old cliché & reclassify new cliché. The marriage of the telegraph & press created the front page of the daily newspaper with its discontinuous juxtaposition of images.

Hot-liners cross public radio with private telephone. Much of the power of this medium derives, I believe, from its newness & is therefore temporary.

Joyce crossed cinema & book in *Ulysses,* radio & book in *Finnegans Wake;* in so doing, he not only threw light on these three media, but he used each as a means of retrieving that wealth of perception & experience stored in the English language.

Crossing tape recorder & book produced the nonliterary autobiography: Oscar Lewis's books, Kramer's *Instant Replay,* etc.

Crossing the tape recorder & still camera & book produced such works as *Black* & Guy Carawan's book on the Sea Islanders.

In the 1968 elections the McCarthy campaign staff was approached with a suggestion for crossing media. In the United States no law prohibits the mating of radio & TV. In Southern California, for example, Spanish-speaking sportsfans watch the picture on TV but listen to a Spanish-speaking sports broadcaster on radio. So it was proposed that the New York-New Jersey area be offered a night of radio sound & TV picture. Five commentators were to provide the audio: John Culkin, Jean Shepherd, Marshall McLuhan, myself & Tony Schwartz, who originated the idea and had a sound studio equipped to handle the project. A bank of small TV sets offered simultaneous coverage of all principal TV stations in the area; each would be kept on its particular channel. From these the commentators would select programs shown on a master TV set & toward these programs would direct their comments. The plan was to announce in the New York-New Jersey newspapers that at 7 P.M. on a certain night a local radio station would provide that evening's TV audio. For example, the audio for a TV cigarette commercial would be one minute of coughing via radio. If there was a laughshow, it would be pointed out that the laughtracks were copyrighted in 1935 & that most of the people one heard laughing had been dead for some time. Then listeners would be asked to turn to a channel showing Walter Cronkite, at which point they would hear a taped "countdown," first in English, followed by an A-blast; then in Russian, then Chinese, each followed by blasts & more blasts & finally only a child's cry. Finally, and this was the point of the whole project, listeners would be encouraged to turn to a channel with Hubert Humphrey speaking. Instead of his speech, however, they would hear—on radio—the four letters he wrote to his draft board gaining exemption from duty in the Second War—one letter citing two lectures he had delivered to an ROTC class, while in the background would be played Hitler's ranting, bombs & screams; then Humphrey's pro-Vietnam War speeches —"A glorious adventure and great fun, isn't it?"—while in the background the guns & screams continued.

The McCarthy team, mostly literary men, saw something profoundly immoral in the suggestion. New forms always seem immoral or chaotic since they are unconsciously judged by reference to consecrated forms. But a curious contradiction arises: new forms are condemned, but the information they disseminate is believed, while the old & valued aren't even seen.

THE TRIBE THAT SWALLOWED THE PRIVATE "I"

Tribal men everywhere regard themselves as integral parts of nature. They belong to a seamless web of kinship & responsibility. They merge the individual with the whole society. They're involved with life: they experience a *participation mystique*. This experience is one in which people are eager to merge with cosmic powers.

Beginning with the phonetic alphabet & the Greeks, there came a habit of detachment & noninvolvement, a kind of uncooperative gesture toward the universe. From this refusal to be involved in the word he lived in, literate man derived detachment & objectivity. He became alienated from his environment, even from his body. He believed there was an elegance in detachment. He valued the isolated, delimited self, especially the mind. He became an island, complete unto himself.

Today we've entered a relatively dim, resonating tribal world in which the electronic extensions of everybody's nerves involve him deeply in all other lives. Where writing & print technology tore man out of the group, creating the great misery of psychic alienation, suddenly & without warning the electronic media hasten him back into the embrace of the group. Electricity binds the entire human community into a single tribe, with much resulting erosion of individualism.

While this threatens the sense of identity of many people, it can also heighten our awareness of the shape & meaning of our lives to the level of extreme sensitivity: Eliot's to "understand what it is to be awake, to be living on several planes at once."

TRIBAL ARTIST

"Art" is a title traditionally reserved for works of self-expression. Aestheticians & art collectors, taking a belated interest in ethnic & electronic art, now accord both fields the dignity of this title on the grounds that both meet this requirement. They refuse to believe "true art" can be achieved, by other means.

But self-expression, a product of literacy, is alien to the tribal world. Everyone in a tribe is involved with everybody, simultaneously. Tribal societies are implosive. There is no isolating individualism, no private consciousness, no private point of view. These are products & goals of literacy. The image of a tribal artist as a specialized, fragmented, role-less individual who seeks to discover himself & to reveal his private point of view, is nonsense. The private wits or senses of men were released from their corporate restraints by the fragmenting power of print. Today we experience this in reverse: the explosive individual energies of literate men are being compressed & imploded by electronic circuitry.

Individualism means fragmentation, self-expression, private point of view. People who fill integral roles have no private point of view; they share group awareness & wear corporate masks.

Tribal man is the conventional role player, the faithful mask wearer. Wearing a mask means to divest, not to express, oneself. A mask or role is not an extension of its wearer so much as putting on the collective powers of the audience. The speaker assumes the collective mask of the image he presents. He manifests a corporate attitude toward life.

Among the Pygmies, writes Colin Turnbull, the solo song doesn't exist "except in the form of lullabies: Their songs may be begun by anyone, no matter what his talent. Leadership . . . shifts from an accomplished to a less accomplished singer with no apparent lessening of support from the whole group. The chief delight of the singers is to listen to the effect of group-produced counterpoint as it echoes through the dark cathedral of the jungle."

"As the American Negro becomes more literate," writes Alan Lomax, "he loses his former ability to improvise collectively, to become part of a many-voiced but unified chorus or orchestra. The shift from the highly original polyphonic New Orleans style to imitative, solo-voiced 'cool' jazz—the changeover from the old-time congregational spiritual to the modern solo gospel songs are merely the two most familiar examples of this trend."

Some writers assert that anonymity in tribal art is a myth, that specialists can identify with confidence works by individual artists. But the marks of identity generally turn out to be details of craftsmanship or minor stylistic innovations. Occasionally, works of specific artists can be identified on the basis of exceptional aesthetic achievement. But even these are not examples of self-expression.

Carver & dancer merely interpret traditional designs the way actors interpret parts. There is a vital difference between variations which maintain the freshness of a style, perhaps bringing it to perfection, and changes which destroy & replace that style. The real question is: does the artist manifest a corporate view of life or offer a private point of view? Does he efface himself & identify completely with large forces, or does he become an innovator who regards his uniqueness as more important than tribal conventions?

"I flew by the nets," said Joyce. Did he mean *past* the nets of family, church & country, or *by means* of them? Literate artists fly past the nets; tribal artists by means of them.

"I'd like to be remembered as somebody who told you something you already know." *Woody Guthrie*

ONE TOUCH OF NATURE MAKES THE WHOLE WORLD KIN

"Is it a fact—or have I dreamt it—that by means of electricity, the world of matter has become a great nerve, vibrating thousands of miles in a breathless point of time." *The House of the Seven Gables*

We owe a great deal to that frog whose croak was heard 'round the world one summer evening in 1800. By jerking & twitching every time a distant lightning bolt flashed through the sky, the dead frog made possible Galvani's momentous discovery: active nerves & muscles generate electric current.

We're all electric generators. Electronic media outer our senses: they extend the human sensorium. That extension is shared: electronic media join us to a common nervous system. Just as a blind man's cane extends his body, providing information a hand or foot might provide, so electric media extend our senses, to a global scale. Our electronic nerve endings now reach every part of the world & we function as humans acting on sense data provided by these electronic extensions. This isn't *metaphor:* it's man's biochemical form.

Electronic media have created a global village where all walls between peoples, arts, cultures come tumbling down like the walls of Jericho. Sight isolates, but sound unites. The American Negro was segregated in the *visual* world of literate man, but in the world of sound, his music & speech became the music & speech of all Americans. Like sound, electricity penetrates walls, dissolves barriers. Segregation no longer has meaning in *any sense:* it survives today like a watch ticking in the pocket of a dead man.

Electricity makes vast amounts of information available to all. Photography is a mass of data in a flash. In this vastly confusing environment, the problem becomes one of data selection & processing, forcing everyone to abandon the position of consumer & become instead a co-producer.

Everyone is forced to play the total field. Decision making, even in its simplest form, becomes highly demanding.

As electric circuitry eliminates scarcity in private & public sectors, we encounter the scarcity that has always haunted the rich: the scarcity of life itself to enjoy the richness provided by nature & achieved by genius. We now possess the means to relieve conflicts bred from hunger & from competition for limited resources. But inner conflicts become more severe, calling for an orchestration of resources in harmony with human faculties. We're only beginning to realize what a tiny slice of human potentialities we now educate.

THE WORLD IS NOW A HAPPENING

Formerly, work was in direct relation to the source of available energy. Man scratched the earth's surface for resources. But electric energy is no respector of geography. It allows us to create our own environments, as certain artists create theirs. Suddenly everybody & everything is involved in transforming the entire environment as a work of art. Theater is no longer on or off Broadway. It's out of doors, in the streets. "All the world's a stage and all the men and women merely players."

ART AS ACT

When we look at a particular work of native art & see the shape of it, we're only looking at its afterlife. Its real life is the movement by which it got to be that shape. Natives often discard carvings immediately after making them.

The concept "art" is alien to most, perhaps all, native peoples. But the thing itself, the act of art, is certainly there, carefully implemented as a dimension of culture. It is not, however, always easy to recognize. Eskimo, for example, don't put art into their environment: they treat the environment itself as art form.

Life-as-art is taken for granted by preliterate peoples, many of whom have no word for "art." Among the Naskapi, hunting is a holy occupation in which artists engage. Sioux walk-in-a-sacred-manner when on a buffalo hunt. The Balinese say, "We like to do all things beautifully."

The Wolof of Senegal go further: they apply the words *tar* & *rafet,* "beauty" & "beautiful" to people; but for art words they use *deveka, yem, mat,* "that is suitable," "that is proportioned," "that is perfect."

In such societies, art is invisible: it belongs to that pervasive environment which eludes perception. It serves as a means of merging the individual & his environment, not as a means of training his perception upon that environment.

In native societies I know firsthand, art belongs to ordinary day-to-day experiences: the way a father addresses his son, decorates his house door, butchers a pig, dances, puts on his loincloth in the morning, or addresses his guardian spirit. When Andy Warhol recently offered to sign any object, including dinners, clothes, & what-have-you, he illustrated a point natives have never doubted: Art & Life are interchangeable.

Suppose Picasso started signing Ford cars, babies, menus, old buildings, photographs? Suddenly art dealers & teachers wouldn't know how to identify art.

Recently when an important New York traffic sign disappeared, Traffic Commissioner Henry A. Barnes speculated: "It's probably hanging around with a Picasso in some Villager's studio."

To put a tomato can in the Guggenheim Museum, or to bring the unintended noises of the ordinary environment into the concert hall, is an important way of announcing that the environment itself is an art form, and that the total human condition can be considered as a work of art.

When art becomes inseparable from daily living— the way a woman prepares a meal, speaks to her children, decorates her home, makes love, laughs— there is no "art," for all life is artistic.

"There is / one art, / no more, / no less: / to do / all things / with art— / lessness." *Piet Hein*

Where art is the human creating of form & order, all man-made rhythms & patterns are art. Language is art & "everyone by whom it lives" is an artist.

"Everything we do is music," says John Cage. "Everywhere is the best seat."

California youth: "Any art I do is something I feel right at the moment. Even dressing this way is art. When you're walking down the street like this, you don't have an exhibit of your paintings, or even say anything."

ART AS ANTIENVIRONMENT

Beginning in Classical times, *i.e.,* the coming of literacy, the arts were set apart from daily living. Impermanent arts like cooking, grooming, gardening weren't highly valued & those who practiced them weren't accorded the title "artist." What was valued was permanent art, generally produced by men. These provided exemplary or visionary models. Constructed as countersituations to daily living, they provided both a comparison & a position from which to examine daily life. They acted in the role of antienvironments, enabling one to perceive his environment with detachment & clarity. "The great quality of true art," wrote Proust, "is that it rediscovers, grasps and reveals to us the reality far from which we live, from which we get further & further away as the conventional knowledge we substitute for it becomes thicker and more impenetrable, the reality that we might die without having known and which is simply our life, life finally discovered and clarified. . . ."

Today what is called Pop Art is the use of some object from our daily environment as if it were antienvironmental. We put it in a museum or concert hall where, for the first time, we perceive it. Pop Art serves to remind us, however, that electronic man has fashioned for himself a world of artifacts & images intended not to train his perception or awareness but to insist that he merge with these artifacts & images, just as the native merges with his environment.

Speech structures the abyss of mental space. It's an invisible architecture of the human dark. "Speak that I may see you." Writing turned a spotlight on the high, dim Sierras of speech; writing was the visualization of acoustic space. It lit up the dark. It gave us the Greek Miracle.

Writing was the first real antienvironment. Plato's Academy & all schools founded on literacy were antienvironments—ivory towers, observatories for detached perception. All people obey rules of grammar, but only literate people are conscious of these rules.

Seeing speech detaches you from it & you can perceive its form. "How do I know what to think," asks Alice, "till I see what I say?"

And how do I know who I am until I see myself? Even seeing one's name can be electrifying. Isak Dinesen tells of recording a deposition for an illiterate Kikuyu: "When Jogona had at last come to the end of his tale, and I had got it all down, I told him that I was going to read it to him. He turned away from me while I was reading, as if to avoid all distractions.

"But as I read out his own name, 'And he sent for Jogona Kanyagga, who was his friend and who lived not far away,' he swiftly turned his face to me, and gave me a great fierce flaming glance, so exuberant with laughter that it changed the old man into a boy, into the very symbol of youth. Again as I had finished the document and was reading out his name, where it figured as a verification below his thumbmark, the vital glance was repeated, this time deepened and calmed, with a new dignity.

"Such a glance did Adam give the Lord when He formed him out of the dust and breathed into his nostrils the breath of life, and man became a living soul. I had created him and shown him himself: Jogona Kanyagga of life everlasting. When I handed him the paper, he took it reverently and greedily, folded it up in a corner of his cloak and kept his hand upon it. He could not afford to lose it, for his soul was in it, and there was the proof of his existence. Here was something which Jogona Kanyagga had performed, and which would preserve his name for ever: the flesh was made of word and dwelt among us full of grace and truth."

Literacy & its attendant technology promoted detachment & objectivity, detribalization & individuality. Electric circuitry has the opposite effect: it involves in depth. It merges individual & environment. Advertising produces effects for the total economy, but doesn't increase human awareness. As in native culture, art-music-ritual are integral parts of the daily sensory environment. In these circumstances, awareness & opposition of the individual are irrelevent & futile.

SERVICE ENVIRONMENTS

Monarchs & millionaires created private worlds with private wealth. Morgan & Astor, imitating European princes, had private libraries, art collections, opera boxes, parks. Both had private Pullman cars, but neither was wealthy enough to own a *private railroad.* Since they administered railways & derived profits from them, they probably suffered from an illusion of ownership. But ownership was essentially public: railways served the public & were financed by passengers & shippers. As Henry Ford pointed out, private profit from technology was negligible compared to public profit.

The moment any service exceeds what any single individual can control, that service is environmental. When environmental services exceed the reach of the greatest private wealth, that society is Communist.

By 1830, *i.e.,* long before Marx, a majority of citizens in England & especially the United States, had moved into service environments: they could avail themselves of postal, shipping, travel, publishing services that not even the wealthiest capitalist or most powerful monarch could possess. Rich & poor, young & old shared this environment. Like all utopias, Marx's was a rear-view mirror.

The short-range view—disparity of profit between capitalist & worker—was easier to recognize & respond to than the far greater factor of total environment change.

All media are environmental. A language is a resource common to all who speak it. The "King's English" meant, not proper English, but the language environment shared by the King's subjects.

Television is part of the only environment today's

children have ever known. To punish a child by forbidding him to watch TV is as nonsensical as threatening to deprive him of heat.

To try to restrict this service environment to white adults, or to regard its benefits as products of private labor, is equally nonsensical. The unemployed Negro youth who demands admission into this environment understands its nature far better than the middle-class white who strives to exclude him.

The unskilled-uneducated-unemployed of 1830 London lacked even minimal resources to participate in the service environment. They lacked not only the penny to mail a letter, they lacked the literacy to write it. They lived in the midst of a service environment, but could not participate in it. Their admission into it was the "Reform Movement" of that day. Today we face a similar challenge: expanding membership in the service environment.

Electronic media have made all the arts environmental. Everyone can avail himself of cultural riches beyond what any millionaire has ever known. Today no serious scholar limits himself to Morgan's Library when the entire New York Public Library is open daily & paperbacks are everywhere at hand. No art lover restricts himself to Morgan's collection. Morgan's estate was nothing compared to any national park, and the cheapest radio offers infinitely more & better music than Morgan ever heard in his exclusive opera box. LP's & magnetic tapes make environmental all music from all times: music, like a wild bird's song, now belongs to the environment.

No one can own an environment: one can only own things *in* an environment. To natives, nature was the service environment. No one owned it. White settlers, believing they had purchased land from Indians, found they had been granted only access to this environment (hence the term "Indian giver").

The moment your environment begins to provide services beyond what a private individual can control, you are entering the state of communism. In this sense, the United States has been communistic for some time, more fully than any other country. Only a bookkeeping smokescreen conceals this fact. America reached this state via technology, not propaganda or revolution.

Today in the United States there are no longer any significant areas of private wealth. The multibillion dollar service environment of electric information is free for all. Knowledge industries are the only significant ones now. Education, news, transportation, entertainment, medicine, arts, telephone are all environmental. J. Paul Getty complained that his riches didn't distinguish him from junior executives who drove the same car, ate the same cornflakes, watched the same TV programs. It wasn't his immense wealth that made him a public figure but his essays in *Playboy*.

We tend to see this new service environment as a variant of the world of private property. Pockets of people persist in the belief that power & pleasure reside in possessions. But the trend is otherwise. Even houses & cars are becoming services. People want clean clothes, not washing machines; transportation, not cars. One California company advertises, "Sell us your car. We'll rent it back to you." Possessions become encumbrances in a world of services. Power no longer lies in private property but in the service environment itself.

MINI-ENVIRONMENTS

Aural, tribal man lives in multiple mini-states, not the big, homogenized state of literate, commercial man.

Print technology, with its attendant mass production of goods & attitudes, produced a uniform, homogenized America where a drugstore in Atlanta was indistinguishable from one in Cheyenne. Only New York City, and only to a limited extent, resisted this: in spite of the uniformity of streets & buildings, one moved in & out of different environments in the course of a brief stroll—hence New York was often said to be "not an American city."

In the past, the sounds & movements of the streets provided the drama of city life. People played out that drama in the streets or watched from windows & doorsteps. Stores displayed wares in windows for passerbys. Stores today are often windowless; their displays are inside. People watch parades on TV; they hear the cries of peddlers on radio. Street sounds have become interference, noise, preventing even conversations out-of-doors. Talking-while-walking is now almost impossible in big cities (will the rhythms of speech change?). The street as a river of commerce

& communication has become a wasteland between mini-environments.

High-rise buildings are mini-environments. No neighborhoods surround them. Each must be governed from within: all efforts at outside control fail, with much resulting abuse of buildings. Kitty Genovese's screams came from *outside;* would they have been ignored if they had come from *inside?*

All over the world, electric media stimulate the rise of mini-states: in Great Britain, Welsh & Scottish nationalism are rescrudescing powerfully; in Spain, Basques demand autonomy; in Belgium, Flemings insist on separation from the Waldons; in Canada, Quebecois are in the first stages of a war of independence; in Africa, we've witnessed the germination of several mini-states & the collapse of several ambitiously unrealistic schemes for regional confederation. These mini-states are just the opposite of the traditional centralizing nationalisms of the past. The later forged mass states that homogenized disparate ethnic & linguistic groups within one national boundary. The new mini-states are decentralizing tribal conglomerates of those same ethnic & linguistic groups.

END & REBIRTH OF EXPERIENCE

Experience is now useless. It's no good at high speed. With speed up of information, practical men become obsolete. Experience isn't enough. Only knowledge avails. "Experience is the schoolmaster of fools."

"Experience is a poor guide to man, and is seldom followed. A man really learns little by it, for it is narrowly limited in range. What does a faithful husband know of women, or a faithful wife of men. The generalizations of such people are always inaccurate. What really teaches man is not experience, but observation. It is observation that enables him to make use of the vastly greater experience of other men, of men taken in the mass. He learns by noting what happens to them. Confined to what happened to himself, he labors eternally under an insufficiency of data." *H. L. Mencken*

Information speed-up reveals form & meaning. Any new technology, *e.g.,* print, going fast around an old technology, releases a flood of perception.

Condensing time & data—speeding up experience —reveals process. Archeology & history are instant playback. All mnemonics is playback of awareness. Art is playback.

Information overload requires speed up which permits recognition. We live in the first age when information is so abundant & change so rapid, pattern recognition becomes possible for every one. Until the present era, this awareness was limited to the artist, who had the power & courage to read the language of the outer world & relate it to the inner world. But today, for survival, every one must become aware of what is happening to him, despite the attendant pain of such comprehension.

Pattern recognition is highly abstract. It requires detachment from immediate, particular sensory, experiences. It renders sensory experience obsolete. Sensory experience is now junk & garbage. As such, it serves as art. We now enjoy a real two-party system: a sensate, tribal world has been re-created as art & today serves as antienvironment to the abstract, nonsensory world of pattern recognition. Young people value intense, extraordinary sensory experiences; dress as Navaho; prepare native dishes; work at handicrafts. "The only thing that matters," says Antonioni, "is experience."

WORLD OF DIVIDED SENSES

Phonetic writing translated, into one sense only, the multi-sensuous thing that is spoken language. The peculiar effect of translating the many senses of the spoken word into the visual mode of writing was to abstract one sense from the cluster of the human senses.

The phonetic alphabet & all its derivatives stressed a one-thing-at-a-time analytic awareness in perception. This intensity of analysis was acheived at the price of forcing all else in the field of perception into the subliminal.

Literacy ushered man into the world of divided senses. The value accorded the eye at the expense of all other senses destroyed harmonic orchestration of the senses, and led to emphasis upon the individual experience of the individual sense. It created a hierarchy of senses with sight the highest, touch the lowest. Aristotle, in the first sentence in *Metaphysics,* says ''of all the senses trust only sight.'' This bias makes no sense apart from literacy. Plato regarded touch as the lowest sense. But do lovers?

The Renaissance reversed the medieval axiom ''Seeing is believing, but to touch the Word of God,'' to ''Seeing is believing.'' Literate man said: ''I'm from Missouri: show me''; ''Believe half of what you see and nothing of what you hear.'' He called touch, taste & smell the ''bedroom'' senses or the ''grosser'' senses. Truth, he held, was to be found with the eye; *Proverbs* warned: ''The Eyes of the Lord preserve knowledge, and He over-throweth the words of the transgressor.'' Even Jesus said, ''See how you hear. . . .''

It took 2500 years to enthrone sight. It was a much-contested ascension (''It is written, but I say unto you''), but literacy won & its analytical bias permeated every aspect of society.

THE CROWDED STAGE

The senses aren't mere input channels: they make their own worlds of spaces & relations.

Every sense has its own paradigm of pleasure & pain, creates its own time & space—is, in fact, a unique environment. Similarly, each medium has its bias, creates its environment, produces its effects. Media interpenetrate & interplay with one another, much as senses do. But the bias of each can be isolated & its effects, achieved separately or in combination with other media, can be studied. Media, like art forms, are models of sensory programming.

Remove an organ from a body & the remaining organs play new roles; add an organ & reorganization also occurs. This is true of media as well: new media recast old media in new roles. The appearance of television, for example, forced all other media to play new roles: radio brought back "theater in the round," classroom seats were unscrewed from the floor, and we all became "wired for sound."

For 2500 years, under literacy, Western civilization was dominated by one medium: language. All truth, it was believed, could be housed inside its walls. Writers attempted to enclose the sum of human experience within the walls of rational discourse; scientists attempted to order reality within the goverance of language. Nonverbal media became subservient to verbal categories.

But the synthesis of understanding which once made common speech possible, today no longer works. As George Steiner points out, large areas of meaning are now ruled by nonverbal languages such as mathematics or symbolic logic or film. Little or nothing is "verbal" in modern music or art. Both are languages, yet nothing can be said about either that is pertinent to the traditional habits of linguistic sense. Absolutely nothing can be *said* about a Franz Kline painting. A De Kooning canvas has no subject of which one can render a verbal account; it bypasses language & seems to play directly on our nerve ends. "Whereof one cannot speak," writes Wittgenstein, "thereof one must be silent."

The same applies to much contemporary dance, film & music, especially electronic music. When we ask the contemporary artist to explain himself, he refers us back to his work. He's reluctant to translate his effort into words, that is, into a wholly different medium. "If I could tell you what it meant," said Isadora Duncan, "there would be no point in dancing it."

"I have defined poetry," wrote Frost, "as 'that which is lost in translation' and nothing is lost in translating Sandburg."

The New Criticism in poetry was based on the discovery of the impossibility to paraphrase.

One cannot translate modern mathematics into words. One cannot even paraphrase. The two are independent systems of notation.

This applies to other media as well. To copyright music, one publishes it, but much contemporary music cannot be recorded visually. It is its own language: "A baby crying in the night/In no language but a cry."

The monopoly, even tyranny, language enjoyed under literacy, was shattered by electricity. Language was once the sole, or at least dominant, actor on stage. Today the stage is crowded. No medium dominates the others. All are free to develop into languages of their own, as articulate & elaborate as those of verbal discourse.

". . . to go on from there, I can't use words; they don't say enough. . . ." *Jefferson Airplane*

We might liken it to the difference between synchronized music played by musicians obedient to a strict conductor, and music with interweaving rhythm patterns played by improvisors, each with his own downbeat.

Certain African musicians carry on five simultaneous rhythms, the melody & four percussion parts. Three rhythms are common in preliterate music: melody, handclapping & tapping the feet; the individual performs all three simultaneously, though not in synchronization.

Most literate men, conditioned to take one-thing-at-a-time, simply cannot do this. But postliterate men can. The gap between generations is a gap between sensory profiles.

Electronic media have eroded traditional individualism, weakened representative government & led to a general loss of those freedoms & protections enjoyed under literacy. The ballot box simply can't create images for the electronic world. Freedom has shifted from government to art. Today's varied media, each a unique codification of reality, offer range & depth for human expression & fulfillment perhaps equal to those abandoned.

Man used tools to unlock the resources of the earth. Now he uses language & art to unlock resources within himself. Mating a language or an art with electricity creates new media of astronomical power. These media aren't toys: they shouldn't be in the hands of Peter Pan executives. They can be entrusted only to new artists, because they are art forms.

Harnessing the Tennessee is kid stuff compared to curbing films or television to human ends. The wild broncos of technological culture have yet to find their busters or masters. They have found only their P. T. Barnums.

THE LIVING TRUTH OF THE HUMAN FACE

Not to speak doesn't mean one has nothing to say. Those who don't may be brimming over with emotions which can be expressed only in gesture & play of features.

Gestures convey inner emotions which would still remain unexpressed when everything that can be told has been told and "words get in the way." Such emotions lie in the deepest levels. Facial expression is human experience rendered immediately visible,

without the intermediary of words.

    Print created the drive for self-expression, self-portraiture (Montaigne, Rembrandt), but in time it rendered illegible the faces of men. Silent reading became thinking divorced from both emotions & body. When speech began to imitate printed language, facial expression fell into desuetude.

    Photography, film, TV, aided us in the recovery of gesture & facial awareness—a language of moods & emotions never adequately expressed in words and totally lost in print.

ALIENATION

Alienation from all senses save sight, led to emotional detachment—the inability to feel & express emotions. Literate man not only concealed emotions; he experienced them less: "Unmoved, cold, and to temptation slow." Psychiatrists tell us that people who can express emotions can more readily experience them & that those who cannot express themselves are ill.

In tribal societies especially, perception or cognition is associated with, or immediately followed by, an "emotion." Every idea is not only a state of knowing but a tendency to movement: "To see her is to love her"; "I shuddered at the thought."

Emotion affects both heart & lungs. "Every emotion quickens the action of the heart and with it the respiration," observed Darwin. "When a fearful object is before us we pant and cannot deeply inspire."

Emotion tends to beget bodily motion. In Homer, the manliest warriors wept openly, beat their chests, tore their hair, and when this was sung about in the Athenian markets, it's probable listeners joined in the expression of these emotions. *Hearing* these accounts meant experiencing them. But one can *read* them without emotion. Any newspaper front page is a mass of tragedies, yet we read unmoved. We could never act nor dance such tragedies without emotion. Nor sing them. Nor express them as poetry. But reading is different. Silent reading is thinking deserted by emotion. It leads to a high degree of separation of mental concepts from the plurality of the concrete.

"I read the news today oh boy / . . . / And though the news was rather sad / Well I just had to laugh." *The Beatles*

"Normal" readers don't get emotionally involved in what they read. They enjoy a sensory detachment—an ability to act without reacting. But printed news may turn on an "unbalanced" reader. Accounts of hotel fires may lead to more fires. Oswald, Ray, Sirhan— each saved & pocketed newspaper clippings.

VISUAL BIAS

Literate man divided up the senses and developed separate art forms around each. Writer, musician, sculptor worked independently; rarely was one gifted in two fields. Literate man valued the individual experience of the individual sense, especially sight.

When an octopus stretches out one tentacle, the other tentacles come in. When a dominant sense comes into play, the other senses become junk. For five hundred years, print culture depressed all sensory life except sight. Literate man called painters, poets, and musicians "artists," but cooks, gardeners, and hairdressers were seldom more than servants.

Appearance became everything. Fashion was concerned only with sight. Fashion models looked like manikins: the clothes, not the girl, mattered.

"Clothes maketh the man." Visual values became the mark of civilized man as compared to the values of the barbarian. Eroticism was almost entirely visual. Men became "girl watchers," peeping toms. Literacy produced the Pin up, the Sweater Girl & "falsies," all of which survive now as camp. Today, when lovemaking is primarily by touch & smell, the *Playboy* nude appears as remote as sculpture.

POINT OF VIEW

"Point of view" became obsolete with electricity. Just as one can receive & process many sounds from many sources simultaneously, so computers process information from many tapes simultaneously. Having a "point of view" means being visually oriented. It means focusing on a particular, forcing everything else into the subliminal.

Under electricity, point of view gave way to total awareness. Point of view survives today like the pin up, among the aged & the isolated.

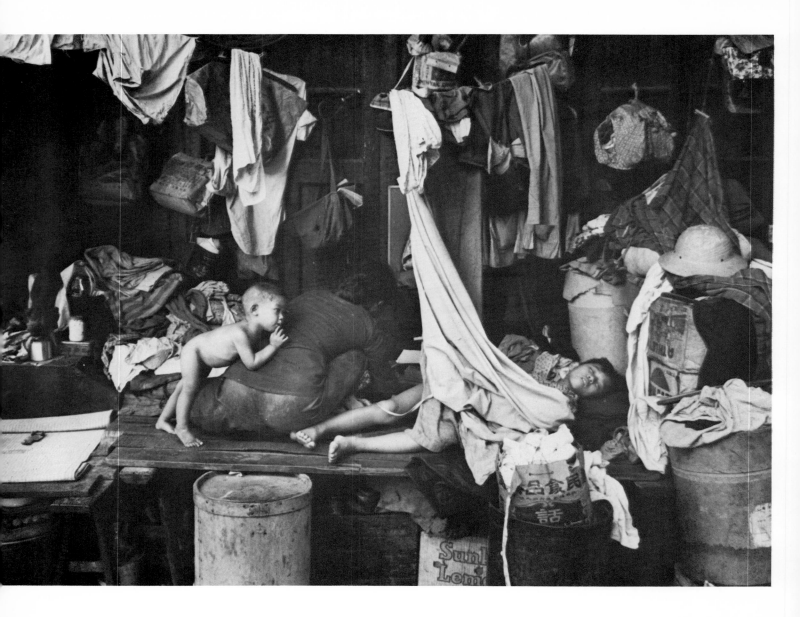

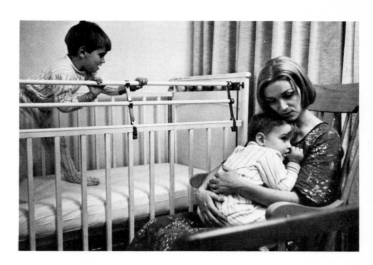

EXPERTS ARE PUZZLED

Point of view = 1°; through the vanishing point = 360°.

Literate man cultivated a point of view, a fixed observation post. He said, "From where I stand. . . ." He pinpointed, divided, abstracted all experience into minute *part*iculars. He divided problems into subjects, projects into committees. This makes no sense to youths today who approach all problems directly on all occasions. They see at a glance how to achieve peace & begin urban renewal; they see starvation & surplus side-by-side and have no patience with habits of thought that insist on taking one thing at a time, step by step. Chain of command, to them means "chains" or comedy.

"On three occasions he [Mayor John Lindsay] picked up wastepaper out of the gutter and gave it to aides to dispose of in litter baskets. The third time he picked up a piece of paper he gave it to an aide, who passed it to another person. That person, in turn, passed it to still another until the paper had gone through four or five hands. Eventually it reached a small boy, who threw it back in the street."
New York Times

PUTTING ON THE AUDIENCE

Charlie Chaplin put on his audience: he played that audience back to itself.

In New Guinea, dancers with feather headdresses & floral costumes put on the jungle.

Anyone who puts on a uniform or wears a mask or plays a role, divests himself of private identity. To wear a uniform is to assume a corporate role.

A performer steps into a role the way he steps into a costume. He puts on his audience. He *re*-presents that audience to itself. How natural that Californians would elect actors to public office.

"Eisenhower was not a father image, but a mirror image to the mass audience. It was themselves they saw in 'Ike'—their own unwillingness to make enemies, their own cheerful superficiality, their own vanity, their own limitations. The fact that he was a war hero gave the mass audience a moral excuse for identifying with him and seemed to put their enthusiasm on a much higher plane. It was not, however, his competence, but the fact that he was not competent that was the real base of his popularity. For the mass audience, Eisenhower represented an enlarged self in a position of his office. . . . [He was] neither a man of goodwill nor a man of bad will, but a man of no will . . . inert and un-inflected—a piece of chewing gum rolling around in the jaws of history. . . ."
Margaret Halsey

"When Nixon is alone in a room, is anyone there?"
Gloria Steinem

The real star today is no longer the performer, but the public. A public relations man can now mold a public as he used to mold a star. A public is born!

The role an actor plays & the mask he wears are familiar to the audience. Often they are age old. He may instill freshness in them; he may give greater depth to their form; but he must not violate this form by giving expression to a private point of view.

Today the young want roles. Though they may mistake these for private statements (which makes them more attractive), these are corporate roles with corporate images, subject to public definition.

They also seek to experience a *participation mystique* with the cosmos by putting on the cosmos, as in astrology, occultism, light shows, etc.

"Dear God, help me to get in harmony with the music to which you have set this world. . . ."

MEDIA AS CODIFIERS

"When Kennedy's body was brought back to New York from Los Angeles, one of us was at the airport to see it arrive. Standing with a group of reporters, he noticed that they almost all watched the event on a specially rigged television screen. The actual coffin was passing behind their back scarcely any farther away than the small-screen version. On these occasions, the tenuous connections between journalism, written or visual, and the real texture of events usually ruptures completely.
An American Melodrama

By "the real texture" is presumably meant the initial sensory experience, devoid of all resonances & reflections. But why, on this occasion, the "connection" between that event & its image on TV was said to be "ruptured" escapes me. Any medium abstracts from the given & codifies in terms of that medium's grammar. It converts "given reality" into experienced reality. This is one of its functions. Without such structuring & classifying there could be no meaningful experience. The "real" is in no sense immediately given to us. What is given is too complex, too ambiguous, too raw. It must first be cooked. Instincts aid lower animals in selecting & responding to stimuli. Man has culture. Culture is his means of selecting—structuring—classifying reality, and media are his principal tools for this end.

We regard it as "natural" to think in verbal categories, but not in TV categories, yet language is as much a technology as TV.

In TV studios, idle employees watch programs on monitor sets, though the live shows are just as close. Billy Graham reports a higher percentage of converts on closed circuit TV than among those watching him "live."

In New Guinea when a village leader is ignored by his people, the Papuan Government sometimes records his speech on tape, then releases it on radio, to be heard by now respectful villagers, played to them by the village leader himself, probably on his own radio.

In the Highlands of New Guinea I saw men with photographs of themselves mounted on their foreheads, in front of their head-feathers. Friends greeted them by examining the photographs.

THEY BECAME WHAT THEY BEHELD

"Oh, what a beautiful baby!" "That's nothing," replied the mother, "You should see his photograph."

All people imitate their creations. Javanese dancers imitate the jerky movements of Javanese puppets. Jazz singers imitate instruments: "I never sing anything I can't play," says Louie Armstrong, "and I never play anything I can't sing."

Victorians moved like steam engines: the Gibson girl coming through an archway (her bustle a coal car) looked like a locomotive emerging from a tunnel.

Today's fashions imitate our principal creations, which are electronic. Women imitate light bulbs or TV sets: their clothes glow: their hair is luminous. They radiate. They can be turned on or off.

Illumination comes from within. It has no visible source. It's not dependent upon outside energy. Today's women are cordless.

"Is it on?" asked a three-year-old holding a ball-point pen.

Psychologists were recently called to aid a boy who couldn't move or speak unless an electric cord, attached to his body, was plugged in.

California hippie: ". . . one couple I know rarely speak but share the same rhythms with tamborines & drums, as well as with their breathing. These rhythms are the same as the ones their electric fan & refrigerator make."

Rural children dream of lambs & bunnies; urban children dream of cars & trains. But acid heads have visions of electronic instruments and, especially under the influence of "electric drugs," identify with TV sets.

"Daddy, are we live or on tape?" *Five-year-old boy.*

"It took me a long time to discover that the key thing in acting is honesty. Once you know how to fake that, you've got it made." *Actor in Peyton Place*

TELEPHONE

"Hello, Central. Give me Dr. Jazz." *Jelly Roll Morton.*

The telephone is said to be the only thing that can interrupt that most precious of all moments.

Aimee Semple McPherson was buried with a live telephone in her coffin.

I once observed a man walking alone past a public phone which rang just as he passed. He hesitated and then, after the second ring, answered it. It couldn't possibly have been for him.

I called various public phones on streets & in terminals and, when someone answered, as almost invariably someone did, I asked why he had answered. Most said, "Because it rang."

On September 6, 1949, a psychotic veteran, Howard B. Unruh, in a mad rampage on the streets of Camden, New Jersey, killed thirteen people and then returned home. Emergency crews, bringing up machine guns, shotguns, and tear gas bombs, opened fire. At this point, an editor on the *Camden Evening Courier* looked up Unruh's name in the telephone directory and called him. Unruh stopped firing & answered.

"Hello." "This Howard?"

"Yes. . . ."

"Why are you killing people?"

"I don't know. I can't answer that yet. I'll have to talk to you later. I'm too busy now."

VIOLENCE & THE QUEST FOR IDENTITY

William James once wrote that no more fiendish torture could be devised than when you speak, no one answers; when you wave, no one turns; but everyone simply cuts you dead. Soon, he said, there wells up within you such hostility you attack those who ignore you and, if that fails to bring recognition, you turn your hostility inward, upon yourself, in an effort to prove you really do exist.

Violence offers immediate public recognition. This is especially true for "invisibles" who thereby become —instantly—very visible. In 1967, when armed Black Panthers entered the California State Assembly, pandemonium occurred. Even the threat of violence is a powerful force in any quest for identity.

Detribalizing the African slave robbed him of all identity, creating great misery of psychic alienation. Racism brainwashed him of his past, leaving him "Wandering between two worlds, one dead / the other powerless to be born." He became an invisible stranger in a strange land.

Though an estimated one third of the post-Civil War American cowboys were black, on screen they all turned white. The Black was erased from history, unseen in advertisements and admitted to radio & film only in comic form. He made his first appearance on TV.

Today's "invisibles" demand visible membership in a society that has hitherto ignored them. They want to participate in society from the inside & they want that society to be reconstituted to allow membership for all. Above all, they want to be acknowledged *publicly,* on their own terms.

Electronic media make possible this reconstitution of society. But this also leads to a corresponding loss of identity among those whose identity was defined by the old society. This upheaval generates great pain & identity loss. As man is tribally metamorphosed by electric media, people scurry around frantically in search of their former identities, and in the process they unleash tremendous violence.

PUTTING ON THE DOG

Pets don't come in breeds or races; they come in styles. Styles match owners. Pet psychoanalysts counsel pet & owner together on the assumption they share psychic problems.

"We train you to train your dog."

A pet cemetery in Washington, D.C. guarantees that pets owned by Negroes aren't acceptable.

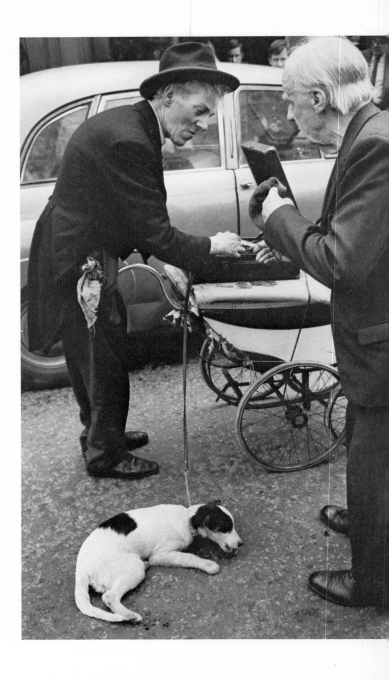

VEHICLES AS EXTENSION OF SELF

"You are what you drive," runs a sports car ad.

The sports car is a wraparound.

Cars are like clothing: the driver locks up his car the way he zips up his fly.

The protecting charm is now worn on the car: Jesus on the dashboard.

In August, the accident rate on Los Angeles freeways is far higher with cars lacking air-conditioning.

"The camel's sure, undulating rhythm transports your body, your blood takes on the rhythm of this undulation, and, together with your blood, so does your soul. Time frees itself from the geometric subdivisions into which it has been so humiliatingly jammed by the sober, lucid mind of the West. Here, with the rocking of the 'desert ship,' time is released from its mathematical, firm-set confines; it becomes a substance that is fluid and indivisible, a light, intoxicating vertigo which transforms thought into reverie and music." *Kazantzakis*

Isak Dinesen tells of a Kikuyu nickname for a keen automobilist: "Half man-half car."

CLOTHING AS WEAPONRY

After the Fall (fig leaf), clothing served as weaponry against a hostile environment.

Clothing also serves as social weaponry. It defines sexes, classes, age groups; fashion is therefore infallible. Violations threaten the social order, producing fear, shock, anger.

Clothing ad: ''Imitation is the sincerest form of battery.'' Youths today mockingly wear Guardsmen uniforms. The ''Lenin cap'' is popular in England. One miniskirt is called ''Hello, officer!'' The Nehru coat & cap were originally prison garb; serving time in a British prison was once a prerequisite for election to public office in India.

In the last stages of the Roman Empire, youth dressed & groomed themselves in the style of the barbarians.

In a society that tries to keep the young "in their place," *i.e.,* invisible, the young have suddenly become very visible. By startling society & getting a reaction, their identity is immediately acknowledged.

Manufacturers supply such weapons because youths now have money and the customer remains a difficult status symbol in our society to degrade. This is, of course, an effective way to neutralize opposition: take over its symbols.

BODY AS SCULPTURE

"In the native world," writes Alan Lomax, "painting lives on the body, sculpture is something you use or worship, architecture you do yourself, and literature you recite or dance."

Grooming & dress are primary arts. Few activities involve more effort. Yet people rarely think of themselves as sculptors or painters, no matter how much effort they devote to making themselves into living art.

In the electronic environment, everyone is constantly bombarded by light images emanating from the cathode tube—Joyce's "Charge of the Light Brigade"—playing on us, going inside us, making us all *The Lord of the Flies,* engulfed by flickering images.

Asked if she had anything on when posing for nude calendar shots, Marilyn Monroe replied, "the radio."

We wear our media; they are our new clothes. TV clothes our bodies tattoo style. It writes on our skins. It clothes us in information. It programs us. Nudity ceases to have meaning. How natural that we would now write ads & headlines on nudes.

DRESS AS CELEBRATION OF IDENTITY

Man is the great pattern-maker & pattern-perceiver. No matter how primitive his situation, no matter how tormented, he cannot live in a world of chaos. Everywhere he imposes form. And the primary form he imposes is himself. Dress is his celebration of identity.

In the mid-winter of 1772, in the desolate Canadian tundra, Samuel Hearne & his native companions saw the track of a strange snowshoe. They followed it to a little hut where they discovered a young woman sitting alone. She told of her capture by a hostile band, of the murder of her parents, husband & infant, and of her escape nearly seven months before. Living alone, without seeing a human face, she supported herself by snaring small game.

"It is scarcely possible to conceive," observed Hearne, "that a person in her forlorn situation could be so composed as to contrive, or execute, anything not absolutely essential to her existence. Nevertheless, all her clothing, besides being calculated for real service, showed great taste, and no little variety of ornament. The materials, though crude, were very curiously wrought, and so judiciously placed as to make the whole of her garb have a very pleasing, though rather romantic appearance."

"The mystery is not that someone should be tossed by chance into this desolate waste": it is, rather, that within this prison of ice & wind, she was able to call from within herself images powerful enough to deny her nothingness.

LOVE MY LABEL LIKE MYSELF

Ortega y Gasset points out, how, in the literate world, the male ego differed radically from the feminine ego in relation to the body. Man's inner sensations were vague, muffled. He forgot his body except in extreme pain or pleasure. By contrast, the female enjoyed a lively inner sensibility. Her senses mixed. Her attention was constantly claimed by inner sensations. Her whole psychic life was physically involved. She was always aware of her body as interposed between her inner self and the outer world; she devoted constant attention to it.

One result was that she appeared to literate man as mysterious. Her body was firm, but filled with tremulous spirit. She created an impression of weakness. The erotic attraction she produced in man was not aroused by her body as body, but by that mysterious spirit permeating it. Literate man spoke of "feminine mystique," "ferminine intuition."

But this inner sensory concert isn't uniquely feminine. In a tribe, it characterizes both sexes: Hence all members adorn & ornament their bodies. Nothing could be more natural. The inner life imposes on every tribal member the habit of noticing & beautifying the body, which ends by being the closest object in the perspective of a person's world. And so tribal members everywhere create that remarkable culture of the body: adornment, cleanliness, and finally, courtesy, that inspired invention which is subtle gesture.

HAIR

Chief Long-hair, a Crow Indian, wound his hair with a strap & folded it into a container which he carried under his arm. It was his sacred medicine & about ten feet long. As this long tress grew, he bound it with balls of pitch placed at intervals of several inches, and on rare occasions released it while galloping on horseback.

Taking a scalp meant acquiring an enemy's power.

Samson's great strength resided in his hair, but Delilah shaved off his seven shaggy locks, unshorn from childhood, thus robbing him of his supernatural strength & rendering him impotent.

In the East Indies, a criminal under torture persisted in denying his guilt until the court ordered his hair cut, at which point he immediately confessed. "One man," recounts Frazer, "who was tried for murder, endured without flinching the utmost ingenuity of his torturers till he saw the surgeon standing with a pair of shears. On asking what this was for, and being told it was to cut his hair, he begged they would not do it, and made a clean breast."

In France, Frazer continues, it was customary to shave whole bodies of persons charged with sorcery before handing them over to the torturer. Millaeus witnessed the torture of some persons at Toulouse, from whom no confession could be wrung until they were completely shaven, when they readily acknowledged the truth of the charge. One woman, who apparently lived a pious life, was put to the torture, and bore her agonies with constancy, until complete depilation drove her to admit her guilt. The inquisitor Sprenger shaved only the heads of suspects, but his colleague Cumanus shaved the whole bodies of forty-one women before committing them all to the flames. He had high authority for this, since Satan himself, in a sermon preached from the pulpit of North Berwick Church, comforted his many servants by assuring them that no harm could befall them "sa lang as their hair wes on, and sould newir latt ane teir fall fra thair ene."

In most preliterate societies ordinary consciousness is associated with the heart & chest, but the early "Indo-Europeans," according to Onians, "believed that the head contained a different factor, the procreative life-soul or spirit, which survives death, and the seed of new life." Among the reasons for thus honoring the head, he cites the analogy with the flower of fruit, seed-pod, at the top or end of a plant; association of sexual experience with sensations & appearances in the head; relating the hair of the head, especially the beard, to pubic hair & to sexual power generally; and finally the association of life & strength with the cerebro-spinal fluid and with the seed that seemed to flow from, and be part of, the latter.

Where the head is considered so sacred it may not even be touched, hair cutting is difficult. There is the danger of disturbing the spirit of the head & the difficulty of disposing of shorn locks to prevent them from falling into the hands of an enemy who might use them mischievously. The simplest way of evading both perils was not to cut the hair at all. From childhood onwards, Frankish kings never chopped their hair. When Clotaire & Childebert converted the kingdom of their dead brother, Clodomir, they sent a messenger bearing scissors & a naked sword to Queen Clotilde, bidding her to choose whether Clodomir's sons should be shorn & live or remain unshorn & die. The Queen replied she would rather see her grandchildren dead than shorn, so murdered they were by their uncle Clotaire with his own hand.

Among the Norse, the hair of thralls was cut short. Ancient Babylonians cut a slave's hair. Among Arabs, what distinguished a freeman was the lock on his forehead, the slave's forehead being shaved. Many religious groups shaved their heads as a symbol of submission.

Jews, shorn & naked, entered gas chambers silently. Military inductees are first shorn: in one swift cut, self-identity is muted. Following the trial of the Chicago 7, the prison warden cut the hair of the prisoners, then exhibited their pictures to a cheering Republican Club. French women who slept with German soldiers were punished by having their heads shaved.

Under literacy, breath, body odors & hair were dissociated from the self, which was sharply delimited. Short hair was required, especially of business & military men: the artist was exempt, but never fully approved. Today the tendency toward long hair is more than social weaponry; it reflects a new self-concept much closer to tribal ones. On the surface the issue seems embarrassingly minor to generate such intense conflict, but in fact its premises are so basic, its emotional roots so deep, that identity itself is challenged.

TO BE UGLY IS TO BE UNSPECIFIED

Cosmetics & clothing advertisers assume everybody
wants to be beautiful. Actually, lots don't. Being
beautiful is being specified. A beautiful woman is
expected to "dress & act accordingly"—that is, to fill a
defined, restricted part. It's a challenge, of sorts, which
not everyone is willing, or interested in meeting. "Leda,
Lada aflutter-afraida, how does your girdle grow?"

Clothing has ceased to be package, container.
It's become an extension of one's skin, of one's inner
character. A woman no longer has to be "with the time"
or "in step with others"; she creates her own time,
keeps step with her own beat.

Today nothing is out because everything is in.
"Nowadays the doorman doesn't know whom to let in."

"That's not clothing: that's clowning." Every costume
from every age is now "junk" & therefore available
as art.

The miniskirt, for example, is a return to ancient
tribal traditions; it's not mere fashion. The kilt is
common in many tribes & was once the comfortable
dress of warriors; it survived into the Renaissance as
the pageboy skirt.

For centuries the power structure kept the middle
class impotent by forcing them to exhaust their limited
resources by buying a succession of new clothes. But
large numbers of youths today reject the consumer
world & the demands it imposes upon them. Sloppy
teen-age attire is, in the main, modest, homely &
comfortable. Many teen-agers make their own clothing.
They tend toward a profound conservatism that
questions the visual tidiness & ceaseless changeability
of their literate elders.

"Clothes bore me," says fashion model Jean
Shrimpton. "I dress very casually, normally, you know.
I just wear sweaters & skirts, mostly, and trousers,
so that I can sit on the floor & relax & be comfortable.
Occasionally I liké to dress up, but ten minutes later I
want to take off what I put on . . . I don't wear kooky
clothes. I wear very plain things. I'm just paid to wear
kooky clothes."

DRESS UNDER DURESS

''Mr. [Henry] Luce is like a man that owns a shoestore and buys all the shoes to fit himself. Then he expects other people to buy them.'' *Governor Earl Long*

Mass production of identical goods required mass consumption by identical consumers. The effect of print was to produce consumer audiences. With the introduction of photoengraving, women pursued the same visual uniformity & repeatability that print brought to men. From this came ''current styles'': the tyranny of Fashion as Fad. Even if a style made a woman look awful, she felt obliged to wear it. She changed uniform on order. Manufacturers could mass produce new styles, confident photoengraving would create a mass demand for them.

Current fashion was like currency: private dress was counterfeit, as unacceptable as a three-dollar bill.

Fashion was obedience to public form. A woman wore one kind of dress or another kind of dress, simply because it was done. By everybody. Not because she wanted to, not from personal selection, but simply because this was what all did. Fashion was a big package deal: Container Corpse of America.

REDISCOVERY OF THE BODY

Literate man valued the delimited, controlling self which he equated with the rational mind. He portrayed this "I" as detached from the body & emotions, and in control of both. He said: *"I* lift *my* foot," with the "I" controlling *me* & *my*. He excluded passions from the "I": these lay below: I *lost* my temper, *fell* in love, *delved* into my unconscious, but I *exercised* my reason.

Early analysts were called "Alienists." Alienation begins when one feels revulsion with one's body, and fears the sensate world. Trudie Shoop, the dancer, helped schizophrenics rediscover themselves by reteaching them the earliest movements of the child.

The story is told of a group of Jews, with downcast eyes, entering gas chambers. One girl, a dancer, was ordered by a guard to dance for his amusement. Naked, shorn of her hair, she had no identity. But as she danced, she rediscovered herself in the dance, in her body: this gave her the courage to act: in a magnificent gesture, she attacked her tormentor.

If you manipulate people, you must first control their environment. Pavlov couldn't make dogs salivate on signal until he put them in artificial, controlled environments. Literate man was easily manipulated. He lived in a centrally heated, air-conditioned, canned-food world, cut off from personal sensations. He was ashamed of his body. He avoided nudity; was obsessed by toilet etiquette; made sex a sin & gluttony close to it. He became aware of his body only in sports & sex, and sometimes not even then.

Today's youths have rediscovered the body. They rebel against all controlled environments; they create personal sensory environments.

Sharp differences between sexes, which marked the past, today disappear. Sex is cooled down. Men & women dress more alike. They share common hair styles. Men wear jewelry. They're interested in lotions, hair dyes, cosmetics. This disturbs older people who keep saying "You can't tell the difference" and then guffaw. Obviously that difference must have meant a great deal to them or they wouldn't be so hung up on this stale joke.

It's a difference that's totally meaningless to the young. Young men & women today share a common sensate world. Their feelings about themselves & about this world are much alike. They can talk together. Sex polarization at social gatherings—so "men can talk, women visit"—is meaningless to the young.

". . . and everybilly lived alove with everybiddy else. . . ."

BEAUTY LIFE IS BODY LOVE

"... and what do you think that pride was drest in?"
Pride of self dresses itself in pride of body. Beauty life
is body love.

SWINGING

When one swings another, or is swung by another,
the centrifugal & centripedal forces create a wholly
new dimension. One becomes inseparable from the
swinger, weightless & in flight. ''How can we know the
dancer from the dance?''

PLAY

In the mechanical, fragmented world of literate man, leisure meant the absence of work, or mere idleness. The reverse is true in the electronic age: the age of information demands simultaneous use of all facilities. Today we are most at leisure when we are most intensely involved, very much as with the artists in all ages.

A job is a fragmented, specialized activity. A man using all his faculties is at leisure or play. The artist doesn't have a job because he uses all his powers at once. Were he to pause to work out his income tax, he would be using only a few of his powers. That would be a "job." A mother doesn't have a "job" because she does forty jobs at once. So with the top executive or surgeon. Under conditions of electric circuitry, all fragmented job patterns tend to blend into involving, demanding activities that more and more resemble teaching & learning & "human service" in its older sense of dedicated service.

"Work" means specialism. It equals fragmented task & consequent noninvolvement of whole person. Play equals involvement, as in hobbies or conversation. Where involvement is low, work is high. Tribal man doesn't work, hence has no need for leisure, no need to re-create whole self. His whole self is already totally involved in living.

Dreams, myths, rituals are all forms of total involvement. The dreamer divests himself of private identity & unites with the corporate image of his group. Tribal Africans are reported to require less sleep than literate wage earners. The nine to five African civil servant needs eight hours sleep, though his physical labor is minimal. What he requires is dreaming. Apparently dreaming is mandatory for human life. Literate man, in dreams, is able to suspend temporarily the unbearable strain of individual identity: he can efface himself by merging with cosmic forces. Tribal man requires less night-dreaming because he achieves this corporate identification through daytime rituals, myths, art, language.

We're reentering the tribal world but this time we're going through the tribal dance & drama wide awake.

SENSATE WORLD OF THE CHILD

Not long ago when some British children were asked
"What are the twelve loveliest things you know?," one
boy answered:

"The cold of ice cream.
The scrunch of leaves.
The feel of clean cloze.
Water running into a bath.
Cold wind on a hot day.
Climbing up a hill looking down.
Hot water bottle in bed.
Honey in your mouth.
Smell in a drug store.
Babies smiling.
The feeling inside when you sing.
Baby kittens."

    A little girl's list went:
  "Our dog's eyes.
Street lights on the river.
Wet stones.
The smell of rain.
An organ playing.
Red roofs in trees.
Smoke rising.
Rain on your cheeks.
The smell of cut grass.
Red velvet.
The smell of picnic teas.
The moon in clouds."

SENSATE WORLD OF NATIVES

When natives talk about their own world, they speak about how things smell, taste, feel, sound: toes gripping roots along a slippery bank; peppery food burning the rectum; "... he became aware of gentle heat playing on his right cheek, and a fine smoke teasing his nostrils, while on the left he heard an odd gurgling sound...."

"It is pleasant," said a Vedda, "for us to feel the rain beating over our shoulders, and good to go out and dig yams, and come home wet, and see the fire burning in the cave, and sit around it."

An Eskimo woman, Uvanuk, delighting in the joy of simply being moved by nature, sang:

"The great sea
Has sent me adrift
It moves me
As the weed in a great river.

"Earth and the great weather
Move me,
Have carried me away
And move my inward parts with joy."

Here the phrase translated "moves me" also means "to be in a natural state"; to be moved by nature is to be in nature, to belong there. Emotions are expressed as physical responses: anger—*loosening bowels;* fear —*tightening sinews;* joy—*floating viscera.* Man is small, no more than a weed moved endlessly by the current, but intensely aware of forces acting upon him, and delighting in even the most trivial.

Toothless Kuilasar, an elderly Eskimo, told of starvation, of children born & husbands lost, of new lands and faces, and concluded, "How happy I have been! How good life has been to me!" She hadn't conquered life, nor been rewarded by it, but life had acted upon her, spoken through her, and this was joy.

SENSORY PROGRAMMING

"Tribal" is a much misused word, favored by critics
of dissident youths. But I mean here neither social
protest nor defiance as a search for identity. I mean
something more basic, something so fundamental, so
total, as to constitute a way of being in relation to life. I
refer to that form of sensory programming best known
from the primitive world, but characterizing the
electronic age as well, where the senses interpenetrate
& interplay, creating a sensory concert or
orchestration.

Consider the Eskimo who, with visibility zero,
navigates his kayak rapidly along dangerous coastlines,
guided by the feel of wind & smell of fog, by sounds
of surf & nesting birds, and particularly by the feel of the
pattern of waves & current against his buttocks. With
such interplay of the senses, there can be no isolation of
one sense. A hunter who relied on sight alone would
return empty-handed; a traveler who ignored odors &
winds & sounds would soon be lost.

The lone Eskimo traveler often dozes on his sled,
facing away from the wind, his parka hood all but
closed. But the fur of the parka, brushing against his
face, warns him of wind changes, and he rouses himself,
checks how the wind is cutting into snow drifts, signals
changes to the dogs if necessary, and then sinks
back into light sleep.

Sir Arthur Grimble tells of a Micronesian who, in a
canoe in the open sea at night, went to sleep knowing
he would feel the direction-current in his buttocks.

Recently an experimenter, comparing paintings by
blind children with those by seeing children, found the
two indistinguishable until the age of six, at which
point the seeing children, being members of a literate,
visual culture, moved in the direction of optical imagery.

Patients who have undergone throat surgery are
forbidden to read, for there is a natural tendency for a
reader to evoke absent sounds, and his throat muscles
work silently as he scans the page.

Nothing was more alien to medievalism than silent

reading. Reading was aloud, often as song, with gestures. Physicians prescribed reading as a form of exercise. Carrels were like telephone booths, designed to keep down noise.

"Sounding-reading" usually includes a sort of dance, a rhythmic rocking of the body—in Mohammedan schools, Jewish *shtetl,* Buddhist monastaries, perhaps village India, too.

Isolating one sense from all others calls for enormous training & self-control and is probably never fully achieved. Test this yourself: run water into the bath while switching the light on & off—the sound appears louder in the darkness.

A child learns to separate the senses when he learns, in class, to read silently. His legs twist, he bites his tongue, but by an enormous *tour de force* he learns to fragment his senses, to turn on one at a time and keep the others in neutral. And so he is indoctrinated into that literate world where readers seek silent solitude, concert goers close their eyes, and gallery guards warn, "Don't touch!"

But all this is history. Today's students mix homework with radio & hi-fi, even TV & telephone, and experience little difficulty correlating such data, or at least having them coexist. California students get into their wrap-around sports cars (a form of clothing), kick off their sandals so they can feel the freeway coming up through the car, travel at 70 mph down the freeway with signs flashing past on the right & the opposite traffic passing at 140 mph; top down; sun & wind in their faces; radio on & every fourth telephone pole in sync with the beat; sharing breakfast with a coed: total sensory involvement. Then they enter class, turn off all senses, put on a tribal face & go numb.

They always remind me of Eskimo sitting silently in an igloo, waiting for clear weather. Early ethnologists suggested that such Eskimo were in self-induced trances. One Freudian said they were suppressing anxiety. In each case it was assumed that an inner dialogue had been displaced. But "conversation with self," far from being universal, is largely a product of literacy. It belongs to literate man whose mind is a never-ending clock which his will cannot stop, sleep suspends only briefly, madness & liquor cannot still, and death alone silences.

Tolstoy & his brother, when they were boys, formed a club, initiation into which required that the candidate stand in a corner for half-an-hour & not think of a white bear.

I don't believe that the silent Eskimo with impassive face is thinking anything. He's just not "with it" where "it" means all senses, action, especially hunting, which he loves above all else. When an Eskimo thinks, he speaks & when he speaks, he moves.

I've seen silent, gentle, slow-moving Eskimo, suddenly caught up in the hunt, accomplish astonishing feats of skill & daring. Yet there was consistency here. They were the same. They simply allowed the world to act toward them with complete freedom. They weren't passive: they freed this experience from its formless state & gave it expression & beauty. When they felt songs welling up within them, they sang; when they felt possessed by the hunt, they committed themselves fully to it.

This sort of electrifying performance always reminded me of slouching Method actors for whom all life is empty dialogue until they suddenly "get with it," "get turned on," erupting with startling jets of power. "Getting turned on" means getting all senses involved, totally. "Freak out" means involvement so complete as to be without any order or control.

"Getting with it" means getting caught up in the sweep of an event or moving under the influence of drugs; it's the warrior possessed by courage; the man who feels an emotion welling up within him; the Eskimo carver letting the ivory have its say. It's the artist possessed by a work in progress as by a fetish with a "life of its own."

"And the time will come," the Beatles sing, "when you will see we're all one, and life flows on within you and without you."

SENSORY ORCHESTRATION

Around 1900, Enos Mills, a mountain guide, became snow-blind in the Rockies at 12,000 feet. "My faculties," he reports, "were intensely awake." He could not use trails because of the depth of snow. Carrying a long staff, he set out on snowshoes to find the blaze marks on trees, which he had made on his forward journey. Making his way from tree to tree he thrust an arm into the snow, feeling the bark on the trees until he discovered the mark of the blaze. He resorted to the trees for the points of the compass. In his study of tree distribution he had learned that, in this locality, canyons running east and west carried limber pines on the wall that faced south and Englemann spruce on the wall that faced north. With limber pines on his left and Englemann spruces on his right he was now satisfied that he was traveling eastward and should be on the eastern side of the range. To check this, he examined the lichen growth of low-lying boulders and the moss which encircled the trunks of trees, concluding that the surrounding area must be such as to admit light freely from all quarters. To get an idea of the topography of the canyon he shouted, noting from which directions the echoes came, their intensity and the cross replies— concluding from these that he was going into the head of a deep forest-walled canyon. In the night a snowslide almost smothered him as he had made his way, and progress was made more difficult by the enormous rock masses and entanglements of fallen branches and leaves. Suddenly he caught the scent of smoke, which he recognized as that of aspen, a wood burned in the cookstoves of the mountain people. Under favorable conditions a person with a keen sense of smell can detect aspen-wood smoke for a distance of two or three miles. Going forward in the direction from which the wind was blowing, he emerged from the woods where the wind was strongest and knew that human habitation was near. In fear of passing it, he stopped to use his ears. As he stood listening, a little girl gently, curiously asked: "Are you going to stay here tonight?"

RESTRAINING SIGHT

"Shut your eyes and *see.*" *Joyce*

"I don't want to live life the way I see it. I'll play my life by ear." *16-year-old New Yorker*

"If you paint, close your eyes and sing. Painters should have their eyes put out like canaries, so they'll sing better." *Picasso*

"There's more than the eye can see...." *Popular Song*

Restraining sight increases awareness through other senses: in darkness, sounds seem louder, odors stronger, flavors sharper & surfaces more vivid. The Blues singer closes her eyes; the ballad singer assumes that blank-faced, blind-eyed expression Lomax calls the Eurasian Style of singing: "... his eyes are closed, or he gazes unseeing...."

Lovers close their eyes. "Love is blind."

"Night has come. Now all the problems speak more loudly." *Nietzsche*

Paleolithic man worked in the darkness of caverns, his paintings illuminated by flickering torch: elusive images appeared/disappeared. His art emerged as a direct response to inner light. He employed "the inward eye." He had no concept of three dimensional perspective with a vanishing point in the distance before him. For him, the vanishing point was within himself and he went through it by stepping into his art.

Hans Arp drew his curved, interpenetrating lines, which so closely resemble certain Paleolithic drawings, with half-closed eyes: "... under lowered lids, the inner movement streams untainted to the hand. In a darkened room it is easier to follow the guidance of the inner movement than in the open air. A conductor of inner music, the great designer of prehistoric images, worked with eyes turned upwards. So his drawings gain in transparency; open to penetration, to sudden inspiration, to recovery of the inner melody, to the circling approach; and the whole is transmuted into one great exhalation."

This is the inward quest, the search for meaning beyond the word of appearances; it's the "prophet blinded so that sight is yielded for insight."

"I can't believe *that!*" said Alice.

"Can't you?" the Queen said in a pitying tone. "Try again: draw a deep breath, and close your eyes."

"What do you see," ask the Beatles, "when you turn out the light? I can't tell you but I know it's mine."

In the late 1930's, the Glenn Miller group sang "Close your eyes and visualize," but to the Beatles, this means all senses: "Living is easy with eyes closed."

INNER STRUCTURE

Recently a Dutch anthropologist purchased a New Guinea men's house. When he asked its builders to dismantle & pack it, he found they couldn't crate what they had so skillfully, beautifully created. Planes intersecting at 90°, even rectangles, were alien to them, as were all notions of space as container.

Literate man finds it easy to crate anything, even that which he can't create, because he thinks in terms of space, not place; that is, in terms of outer container, not inner structure.

An Eskimo doesn't mould his igloo from the outside looking in, but from the inside looking out. Working from the center, he builds a series of concentric circles, tapering upwards conically. When the keystone at the apex has been set in place, Eskimo & structure are one. Only then does he cut a small hole at the base, through which he crawls—in effect, doffing his igloo.

Nineteenth century Alaskan Eskimo produced great mobile masks with extensions & hanging parts, like dissected Miró's reassembled in three dimensions. It was once held that these composite affairs were purely the result of material shortage, large pieces of driftwood being rare. But mobile masks coexisted with large, conventional masks, each carved from a single piece of wood. Form came from choice, not limitation.

No borders froze, imprisoned. Instead, each mobile, obedient to an inner impulse, created its own dimensions, asserted its own identity, unhampered by external restraints.

This is the kind of time-space sense held by modern physicists who no longer try to contain events in time or space but think of each thing as making its own time, its own space. For them, each object, each set of objects, engenders its own unique spaces by the relations the objects have among themselves visually or musically. Time & space interpenetrate each other totally. In the same sense, Cézanne recovered the plastic image by which all of the senses coexist in a unified pattern.

INNER TRIP

Government efforts to arouse interest among the young in space travel have largely failed. The underground press ignores the subject. Astronauts are heroes only to the middle-aged. For the young, the inner trip supplants outer travel. It's the psychic leap of this century; space travel is just a delayed achievement of the seventeenth century. The young are concerned with inside activities, not outside activities.

Just as the Orient is becoming Westernized under the impact of our war technology, so we're becoming reOriented under the impact of electronic media. We no longer think of reality as something outside ourselves, something there, to be observed, measured. This concept came with the Greeks, with literacy, and it goes with literacy, with the coming of the electronic media. Once more, after an interval of 2500 years of literacy, reality is conceived as being within one. The search for truth has once more become an inward trip.

Natives widely believe that the essence of a person, song, object resides within, not on the surface, not in outward appearances. Truth is therefore sought via an inner quest—either within one's self, say in meditation; or in LSD; or through x-ray penetration of the outer world—in the sense that scientists reject appearances, insisting that reality isn't in them but in the laws that govern bodies; or in the sense that Picasso, to show us a total being, takes us right inside.

From this comes the belief that the world consists of bodies, each containing within itself an essence, power, vital energy, which, under certain conditions, is given out, illuminating, changing whatever it touches. When such energy meets forces radiating from another being, something new may be created. Similarly, forces from other beings may penetrate one, enter one, change one. One may "drink in" another. Be possessed by another. Become *in*spired.

INNER EXPERIENCE

Coleridge, De Quincy, Baudelaire, Rimbaud used drugs to dislocate perception & reorganize their imaginative lives. They wanted to get out of the boundaries & patterns of perception as they experienced it in their own culture in order to discover new images. They all had the ambition to discover new worlds of perception, new worlds of sensibility.

"We were the first who ever burst into that silent sea." *Coleridge*

In many tribes the youth seeking insight goes apart from his fellows & lives for a time in the wilderness, fasting & praying.

"If he is the proper sort, he will return with a message from the god he set out to seek, but even if he fails in that particular, he will have had a vision or seen a marvel—and these are always worth listening to and thinking about."

When natives tell of such experiences, they rarely mention things seen. They refer to experiences felt, to "inner voices." Clearly, such experiences aren't primarily visual. *In*sight is more appropriate than "vision"; *hearer* or *feeler* is more accurate than "seer."

"I see things I wish my eyes could see." *Vanilla Fudge*

STEP RIGHT IN

It's not enough to say of x-ray design that it shows both inside & outside of a figure simultaneously. The question is, what does it mean to go right *inside* a form —to be "in the belly of the beast"? I suspect it's something like Alice going through the looking glass, or a Zuni patient stepping into a sand painting, "rolling in it," as it were. You enter, become one with what is portrayed. You are *"in* the know." Notions of detached observation are meaningless here. Jonah & Ahab saw that whale in different ways.

The knower as actor and the knower as observer behold different worlds & shape them to different ends.

In order to know the illness *inside* a patient, a physician must "see through" the patient, that is, *dia-gnose*. In some psychotherapy, the therapist, through semi-hypnotic recall, re-enters the traumatic experience of the patient; he *lives* it with the patient. Similarly, in tribal shamanism, an alien spirit enters the body of a living thing, generally a person. It goes right in & takes over temporarily.

"When I'm *in* my painting," wrote Jackson Pollock, "I'm not aware of what I'm doing . . . there is pure harmony, an easy give and take, and the painting comes out well . . . I have no fears about making changes, destroying the image, etc., because the painting has a life of its own. I try to let it come through. It is only when I lose contact with the painting that the result is a mess."

You come to know a thing by being inside it. You get an inside view. You step into the skin of the beast and that, precisely, is what the masked & costumed dancer does. He puts on the beast.

Characters in native arts & myths are bewilderingly both men & animals. Members of certain totemistic clans assert they are one with the animals from which they claim descent; some expressly declare themselves to *be* the animals in question. Tribal myths contain many references to sexual relations between man & mythical beasts.

A Tlingit myth relates how two brown bears climbed a mountain to escape drowning in a flood. Hunters killed one and took its head & skin to wear as a family crest during festivals. Another Tlingit legend describes how an ancient ancestor was captured by a bear & forced to marry her. When he finally escaped, he took a bear design as his family emblem.

This bear design served as a Tlingit house front on the Northwest Coast, *circa* 1840, and probably before. A gaping hole at the bottom was used as an entrance to the living quarters: one entered the bear through the vagina.

The sensation of entering a woman, being in her, is seldom expressed openly but is everywhere a subject of preoccupation. Parallels between this Tlingit house & a Tingueley "happening"—a huge, reclining female figure one entered— may be more than superficial.

In many ways it's like entering a Bridget Riley walk-in, or a Light Happening ("Step right in," begins Allan Kaprow, or a performance where everyone participates *in* art.

"I wanted," recalls Miró, "to penetrate into the spirit of objects. I realized the cubists had made a great revolution, but it was strictly a plastic revolution. I wanted to go beyond the plastic aspect, to get into the spirit of the thing."

INVISIBLE

". . . the patriotic Archbishop of Canterbury, found it advisable—"

"Found *what?*" said the Duck.

"Found *it,*" the Mouse replied, rather crossly; "of course you know what 'it' means."

"I know very well what 'it' means when *I* find a thing," said the Duck; "it's generally a frog or a worm. The question is, what did the Archbishop find?"

Literate man always felt better when *it* was visible. Language—at least literate languages—favored the observable & measurable. Even early mathematics dealt with the material. Newton was first branded a medieval mystic when his theory of gravity presented a nonvisual bond & reversed downward gravity (*i.e.,* collision) by outward gravity. However, his very visual example of a falling apple made his theory quickly acceptable to the many.

Before scientists turned to higher mathematics, they worked largely within the confines of verbal categories, which were, in turn, rooted in the empirical. *The Origin of Species* was essentially a literary work whose acceptance derived largely from the force of its literary persuasion. Darwin & company limited themselves to how birds & turtles *looked*. "A fine gentleman, but daffy, you know," his gardener said of him, "he stands looking at a flower for an hour, never moving."

No wonder it took twenty-five years before the significance of Mendel's discovery was recognized.

Beginning around 1900, science shifted away from the empirical to the invisible. As early as 1874, in an address to the British Association for the Advancement of Science, John Tyndall said ". . . I cannot stop abruptly where our microscopes cease to be of use. Here the vision of the mind authoritatively supplants the vision of the eye."

Scientists ceased to be interested in the appearance of things & concentrated on the rules which govern them.

Buckminster Fuller writes: "In World War I industry suddenly went from the visible to the invisible base, from the track to the trackless, from the wire to the wireless, from visible structuring to invisible structuring in alloys. The big thing about World War I is that man went off the sensorial spectrum forever as the prime criterion of accrediting innovations. . . . All major advances since World War I have been in the infra and the ultrasensorial frequencies of the electromagnetic spectrum. All the important technical affairs of men are invisible. . . ."

Even government has become invisible. We speak of the CIA as the "invisible government." What could be more natural in a society where truth is regarded as invisible, inner structure?

" . . . IN . . . "

Cellophane initiated "see-through" in packaging: people could see what they were buying. It was the beginning of the end of packaging.

With cut-out, see-through clothing, the eye & mind are no longer arrested at the surface. One enters, becomes one with, the person observed. Sight alone is employed, but all other senses are evoked. It's not the experience of detached observation: one embraces, enters.

"The stage is our bed and the audience is our broad. We're not entertaining, we're making love."
Jefferson Airplane

WAITING, NOT WITH PATIENCE NOR IMPATIENCE, BUT WITH EXPECTATION

Jesse Moses, a Delaware Indian, described his fellow tribesman, Nekatcit: "He was not a smoker. But when he had come into the house, made the greeting and taken a seat, he would either suggest that we have a smoke, or just ask for one. . . . We usually spent about ten minutes just sitting and smoking. . . .

"He explained this period of silence and smoking together as essential, for, said he, 'See, our smoke has now filled the room; first it was in streaks and your smoke and my smoke moved about that way, but now it is all mixed up into one. That is like our minds and spirit too, when we must talk. We are now ready, for we will understand one another better."

In such societies, children are raised to listen to silence as well as sound. Luther Standing Bear, describing his childhood as an Ogalla Dakota in the 1870's, wrote: "[Children] . . . were taught to sit still and enjoy it. They were taught to use their organs of smell, to look when apparently there was nothing to see, and to listen intently when all seemingly was quiet."

Prince Modupe, writing of his childhood in French Guinea, says "We learned that silences as well as sounds are significant in the forest and how to listen to the silences. . . . Deeply felt silences might be said to be the core of our Kofon religion. During these times the nature within ourselves found unity with the nature of the earth."

WINDOW ON CHAOS

"Firelight," writes Isak Dinesen of the Kikuyu, "was not really needed for the dancing, for the moonlight of the African Highlands is marvellously clear and white; it was brought to create an effect. The fire made of the dancing place a stage of the first order, it collected all the colours and movements within it into a unity."

Firelight doesn't dispel darkness: it illuminates things within it. Darkness remains. In masked rituals by firelight, forms appear, then disappear, merging once more with nothingness. Form is temporary. Darkness & silence are constant.

The interval may serve as a reminder of the universal vacancy that everywhere underlies human order.

For centuries the Dogon of West Africa entrenched themselves in the center of the great bend of the Niger, on the fringe of an immense rock plateau. They built their villages, a strange huddle of terraced houses & granaries, all with thatched & pointed roofs, from the debris of the cliff's rock-falls & landslides. "Looking down from above, from the brink of the plateau, is to see a fantastic lunar landscape. All colour has vanished, and even contours are obliterated in waves of heat. Beyond, stretching away as far as the horizon itself, there is nothing visible but a plain of sand, dotted sparsely with bushes. The first impression is unforgettable."

One is reminded of the Hopi of Arizona. Both groups found refuge in unwanted lands—harsh deserts where subtle colors change with the light and homes blend into the landscape. Nothing stands out save man-made art: angular, geometric, hardedged. There's nothing gentle about such art: it's an absolute denial of formlessness. Hopi & Dogon masked rituals break the emptiness of the landscape as abruptly as the blinking neon lights of Las Vegas in the Nevada desert.

EMPTINESS

Convinced that Americans fear emptiness more than fines, a Justice of the Peace in Battle Creek, Michigan, devised a remarkable sentence: he forced traffic violators to sit alone in empty rooms for three to five hours. Outraged citizens made him abandon this punishment, which was regarded as unnecessarily cruel.

When we have a free day, we look forward to how we will fill it. A person who is unemployed must explain: he is ill, retired, seeking work. To do nothing is indefensible. Millionaires expect their children to work during school vacations. Welfare workers are made uneasy by Indians sitting in front of gas stations, and when we come upon an unoccupied child, we say, "What, doing nothing? Do something!"

Literate man regards silence as empty of value. He calls radio silence "dead air" & condemns any cocktail party marked by long silences. Silence in music is usually interrupted by applause from someone who mistakenly thinks the concert is over. A Gilbert Stuart portrait of George Washington, its background unfinished, sells for far less than an identical portrait with background complete.

Dorothy Lee writes: "In Western thought—and I speak here of the view of the unsophisticated—space is empty and has to be occupied with matter; time is empty and to be filled with activity. In both primitive and civilized nonWestern cultures, on the other hand, free space and time have being and integrity. It was this conception of *nothingness* as *somethingness* that enabled the philosophers of India to perceive the integrity of nonbeing, to name the free space and give us the zero."

Writing of the Bedouin tribesmen, T. E. Lawrence tells how one of them took him through a deserted palace where each room had a different scent, and then called "Come and smell the very sweetest scent of all" and led him to a gaping window where the empty wind of the desert went throbbing past. "This," he told him, "is the best: it has no taste."

INTERVAL

An alternate to the art of connecting events is the art
of the interval. Oriental art doesn't use connections, but
intervals, whether in flower arrangement or Zen poetry
or dress. Free time & space are perceived as the
meaningful pause. "Our grandmother did to silence,"
writes Pada Pereva, "what inflections do to a voice."

Practically every aspect of Japanese life asserts the
integrity of the interval. The *ma* ("spaces between"
objects in the scene or simply "spacing" of objects)
and *kukan* ("empty space") are integers, realities.

Emilio Lanier writes: "The key to Japanese culture
lies in the asymmetrical intervals: spacings, rhythms of
writing, designing, music, dancing, all arts. Above all it
lies in the ability to see and *feel* space. . . . The *ma,*
perceived as an area of change—of hue, brightness,
shape—becomes symbolized in all sorts of gestures,
idioms, etc., throughout all of the cultural and practical
arts, and comes finally to be symbolized even more
abstractly in some contexts of activity as the area of
'freedom.' This concept of 'freedom' possesses
a non-Aristotelian dimensionality quite outside the
comprehension of the West, which considers itself the
chief authority on, and author of, liberty and freedom
of every form."

In contrast, practically every aspect of Western
life asserts the exclusive integrity of things, objects,
masses. Spaces between objects aren't perceived as
integers at all; the ideal in technological machines
which yield power, and in Art & Life as well, is to negate
& nullify intervals into rhythmical, balanced, symmetrical
patterns—all exactly alike. According to the Western
"Principle of Plentitude," the universe is full: there are
no gaps, no intervals: "Nature abhors a vacuum"—at
least, Western *human* nature does.

In Japanese flower arrangement, *shuji,* in the rhythm of the tea server in *ocha,* in all the arts of design, in *Noh* & *Kabuki* drama, the interval is stressed. It calls for more participation, being incomplete.

Misako Miyamoto writes of the Noh plays: "The audience watches the play and catches the feeling through not only the action and words but also the intervals of the period of the pauses. . . . There is free creation in each person's mind . . . and the audience relates to this situation with free thinking." Of silent intervals in speech, she says, "Especially [in] the pauses in a tone of voice, I can feel the person's unique personality and his joy, sorrow and other complicated feelings." On listening to a robin in early spring: "It sang with pauses. . . . I could have time to think about the bird [in] in the silent moment between one voice and others. . . . The pauses produced the effect of the relation between the bird and me."

The interval invites participation: it creates riddles that involve one.

"You must enter in
To the small silences between"
  John Moffitt, *To Look at Nothing*
In the allsense-all at once electric world, the interval—not the connection—becomes the crucial technique in organization.

Symballein (to throw together) means to juxtapose, to put together without connections: it implies interval & resonance.

It was in symbolist poetry & in the primary musical structures that the Western world first intuited the onset of the electronic age & the changeover to the art of the interval. Soon there was a tendency for all arts to approach the condition of music: *i.e.,* the art of timing & interval.

Joyce in *Finnegans Wake* took over the art of the interval as a means of retrieving that fantastic wealth of perception & experience stored in ordinary language. As used by Joyce, dispensing with the storyline became the means of instant grasp of complex wholes.

HARDEDGE

"To the blind, all things are sudden." Test this yourself: move about the room with your eyes closed. All encounters become abrupt. Emptiness combines with sudden interface. Connections are lacking; the gradations, shadings & continuities of the visual world are gone.

When Gertrude Stein became acquainted with Picasso in Paris around 1905, he asked her to obtain American comic strips for him. He was studying Japanese prints at the time, but found in comic strips clearer examples of interface & interval which interested him so much. It was at this same period that he began the study of African tribal art.

Most tribal art is hard-edge art. It's art of sharp contrasts, sudden juxtapositions & super-impositions. So is children's art. It favors the strongly marked boundary lines of the icon. Gradation & continuity are shunned.

A film maker in Canada provided young children with the means to make animated films. The result was nearly two hundred films of WHAM! BANG! with figures appearing, disappearing. There were no characters in the ordinary sense; no gradations; no chiaroscuro; just abrupt encounters á la Batman of hardedge, cartoon art.

Hardedge art is a visual presentation, but the experience it evokes isn't visual: it's tactile. It's full of abrupt encounters, sudden interfaces. When you have interface, you have Happenings. In the World of Happenings, surfaces & events collide & grind against one another, creating new forms, much as the action of dialogue creates new insights. It's a world of all-at-onceness where things hit each other but where there are no connections.

SOFTEDGE

"At first sight" the world looks like a flat extension of meaningless patches of light, dark & color jumbled into a quilt-work. Infants born without arms & legs can never see in depth. Depth is discovered by touch, then married to sight. The eye caresses *over* objects.

Tactility converts the flat world of sight into the three-dimensional world of bodies. One by one objects grow out of this chaotic world, and remain unmistakably separate once identified. Patients, blind from childhood, on whom vision has been bestowed by an operation, at first shrink from the welter of additional stimulation & from the flat continuity of the world they see. In 1964, in Sicily, five brothers—all blind from birth—each acquired sight following operations: months later a picture was published which showed them holding on to one another, with downcast eyes, as the lead brother felt his way through the doorway of their home. It took time & effort before they once more recognized the objects around them as separate items.

Only sight offers the sense of flat continuity & connectiveness, and only the phonetic alphabet stresses the sense of sight over all senses. Softedge art, that is, three-dimensional perspective & shading, has its musical counterpart: the acoustic continuity of symphonic music.

By contrast, hardedge art belongs primarily to touch. It stresses interface & interval. The eye is offended by the interval.

Over the entrance to his academy, Plato carved, "Let no man enter who has not studied geometry." By this he meant the lineal, continuous world which his friend Euclid had defined. He meant the literate, visual world of gradations & continuity.

Bishop Burnet, who died in 1715, was disturbed by the unsymmetrical arrangement of the stars: "What a beautiful hemisphere they would have made," he exclaimed, "if they had been placed in rank and order; if they had all been disposed in regular figures . . . all finished and made up into one fair piece, or great composition, according to the rules of art and symmetry."

Sight is the only sense that offers detachment. This detachment gave literate man enormous power over his environment, but led to a corresponding unwillingness to get involved. Man became a detached observer, a passive peeping tom. He stared out from a fixed observation post ("from where I stand") & hoped the view would be unbroken & symmetrical.

INTERPENETRATION

X-ray depicts (simultaneously & without favoritism)
many dimensions of a *single* being. But interpenetration
depicts (simultaneously & without favoritism) *many*
beings. All are locked together: they embrace. No form
overshadows any other. Nothing dominates the
foreground: in fact, there's neither foreground nor
background.

When the Paleolithic sketches at Pech-Merle Cavern
first became known to art historians, these were judged
to be interesting but deficit efforts by artists not fully
human. Thanks to Hans Arp & others, today it's possible
to see these interpenetrating designs for what they are:
superb depictions of the essence of tribalism. In fact,
how else would one depict a tribe?

I put this problem to students: sketch the seamless
web of tribal life, showing the interpenetration of equal
figures, including ancestors. Most were baffled: those
who succeeded did so by producing drawings identical
to native ones.

Literate man generally defined an object in terms of
the unique space it filled, as well as its relations with
objects occupying other spaces. For him, each object
occupied its own space & no other. He perceived the
world as made up of private spaces. In it, every man &
every thing was an island.

JUXTAPOSITION

"A line," says Miro, "has to breathe. If it doesn't, it's dead, and if you can see a corpse, you can smell it."

A basic belief common to both pre- & postliterate men is that powers reside in all things: words, objects, songs and, particularly, people. Under certain circumstances, these unfold themselves or are released, creating change, especially when they transact with energies emanating from other properties.

Hopi farmers don't grow beans: they relate to beans so as to release the bean-ness within each seed—and thus food comes into being.

Physicists tell us that electricity isn't something conveyed by, or contained in, anything, but the conditions we observe where there are certain spatial relations between things.

Symbolist poets juxtaposed words so that energies within each reflected on the other, creating new forms. Rimbaud called these *Illuminations*. Illumination came from within.

Rouault wasn't concerned with the Renaissance technique of "light on," but with "light through"—light emanating from the object & directed *toward* the viewer, as with stained glass windows or television. This calls for total illumination from within & converts viewer into screen.

Translation, even on the dialect level, unlocks powers in language & art imprisoned by classification & convention. Yeats, Joyce, Shaw (Irish) unlocked English, as did Conrad (Pole), Nabakov (Russian), and Pound & Eliot (Americans). Poets unlock powers within words by repositioning them so they transact with one another in new ways.

"Poetry," wrote Laura Riding, "is an attempt to make language do more than express; to make it work; to redistribute intelligence by means of the word. If it succeeds in this, the problem of communication disappears. It does not treat this problem as a matter of mathematical distribution of intelligence between an abstract known and unknown represented by a concrete knower and not-knower. The distribution must take place, if at all, within the intelligence itself. Prose evades this problem by making slovenly equations which always seem successful because, being inexact, they conceal inexactness. Poetry always faces, and generally meets with, failure. But even if it fails, it is at least at the heart of the difficulty, which it treats not as a difficulty of minds but of mind."

COEXISTENCE OF CONTRARIES

The Aztecs devoted themselves to art & torture simultaneously. The extent of human sacrifice among them shocked even hardened Spaniards. In one ceremony, priests incensed a girl who personated the goddess, threw her on her back, cut off her head, caught the gushing blood in a tub & sprinkled it on a wooden image of the goddess. Then they flayed the headless trunk. One of their number squeezed himself into the bloody skin and, clad in the girl's robes, a miter on his head, a necklace about his neck & feathers in his hands, he skipped & postured at the head of a procession as briskly as he could, inconvenienced as he was by the tight & clammy skin.

　　On another occasion, the elders of a tribe which had sent the daughter of their royal house to marry a prince arrived to find a priest dancing in her skin.

　　This was done by the Aztecs, whose guardian spirits spoke to them in the twittering voice of a humming bird, who built a glorious city off the water & who loved to arrange flowers. The contrast struck the historian Prescott so forcibly he suspected divergent strains in their culture, but what made him think cruelty & love of beauty are incompatible?

ARTICULATING THE UNSPEAKABLE

Literate opinion has always refused to acknowledge openly certain forms of human behavior. This refusal may be a virtue but, like many virtues, involves wilful blindness & hypocrisy. It does nothing to reduce violence, obscenity, cruelty. It merely frees them from moral control, leaving their celebration to the irresponsible.

The argument of the censor—that whatever is permitted in art is thereby promoted in behavior—is unproven. Heinrich Pommerenke, who was a rapist, abuser & mass slayer of women in Germany, was prompted to his series of ghastly deeds by Cecil B. De Mille's *The Ten Commandments*. During the scene about the Jewish women dancing about the Golden Calf, all the doubts of his life became clear: women were the source of the world's troubles & it was his mission to punish them. John George Haigh, the British vampire who sucked his victims blood through soda straws, first had his vampire longings from watching an Anglican Church service.

Many tribal myths & rituals offer serious orientation to behavior rarely encouraged or even tolerated in daily life, including imitations of insanity in shamanistic rites. At least one modern parallel is striking: when Elvis Presley stands with head tilted to one side & slightly forward, hair falling over half-closed eyes, his body wracked by spasms while he rhythmically caresses one thigh or arm, this is as good an imitation of catatonia as most actors could offer. The audience understands; it shouts approvingly, "Crazy, man! Wild! Mad! Way out!" It is, of course, a voluntary act, turned on & off as programmed. If it continued after the program, the audience would be less approving.

NO HIDING PLACE

The phonetic alphabet & all its derivatives stressed a one-thing-at-a-time analytic awareness in perception. This intensity of analysis was achieved at the price of forcing all else in the field of perception into the subliminal. For 2500 years literate man lived in what Joyce called "ABCED-mindedness." He won, as a result of this fragmenting of the field of perception & the breaking of movement into static bits, a power of applied knowledge & technology unrivaled in human history. The price he paid was existing personally & socially in a state of almost total subliminal awareness.

In the present age of all-at-onceness, we have discovered that it is impossible—personally, collectively, technologically—to live with the subliminal. Paradoxically, at this moment in our culture, we meet once more nonliterate man. For him there was no subliminal factor in experience; his mythic forms of explanation explicated all levels of any situation at the same time. This is why Freud makes no sense when applied to pre- and postliterate man. That center of anxiety, the subliminal world literacy left vacant & haunted, electricity has invaded like light. We are all post-Freudians.

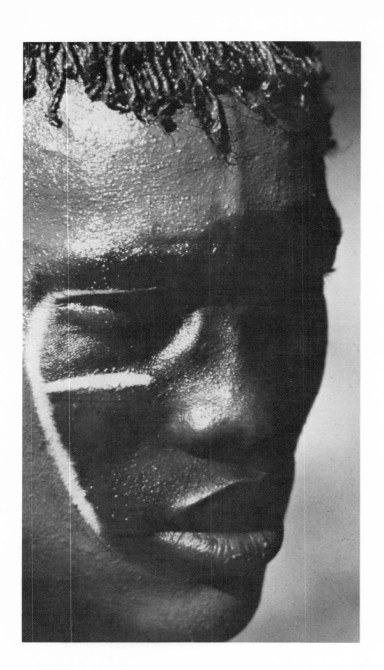

EYE BEAM

Natives generally regard the eye as both transmitter & receiver. Many hold that a luminous quality goes from the eye into what it sees.

Village Greeks today openly stare: they want to look you in the eye, in the same way they openly eavesdrop! All reject you by not wanting to see or hear you.

In early Greek, "to look at" meant *to breathe at;* "perceiving" meant *taking in.* "Check thy dread eye and the blasts of thy breath," warns Euripedes. Plato believed sight was the result of "fusion of rays, the light of the eyes flowing out some distance into the kindred air and the light from objects meeting it."

Such theories had their analogy with children who equate *seeing* & *giving light.* For very young children, seeing is partly outside the eye. It comes from the eye, it gives light, and they're puzzled why they don't feel it. Boy of five: "Daddy, why don't our looks mix when they meet?"

No handier illustration exists than comic books. Superman's heat vision can paralyze an enemy, penetrate concrete, melt a safe, cook a hot dog. When his look meets Superwoman's look, a flash occurs at the point of impact.

The notion that looking is a generative force, that the meeting of two looks can be creative, is widespread. According to Freud, blindness symbolizes castration: hence blinded Oedipus leans on a stick, the stick being a phallic symbol.

The Bambara of Africa say it's by the eyes, as well as the sexual organs, that a wife is united to her husband during intercourse. Defective children, they say, are those conceived during intercourse when the eyes are closed. One is reminded of the Hindu tale of the man who offended a god & in punishment was made so ugly that his wife kept her eyes closed during intercourse, as a result of which their child was born blind.

Until the seventeenth century, the Western world thought of the eye as a broadcasting station, a center of diffusion & emanation from the pupil or the "apple of the eye." "Keep me in your eye" (Psalm) meant: *Keep me in existence, God; Don't let me off your radar screen.* "Laid eyes on" meant *to call into existence;* "overlook" was a verb associated with the evil eye. The eye was assumed to be the organ of action, the ear the organ of reception. Gradually, under literacy, the sense ratios altered & the eye came to be regarded as a means of passive pickup of experience. That trend has suddenly been reversed: the ancient notion that the eye is an organ of power is once more being expressed.

AVOIDANCE OF STARE

Ethnologists in the field find it sound practice never to stare. Many tribesmen regard the eye as an organ of will, not reception. The evil eye is greatly feared.

In conversation, natives generally look to one side or down, a habit Westerners regard as shy or sly. Literate man values the person who "looks one right in the eye," but to a native there's something baneful in the direct glance; one who stares at another is considered as planning, or actually to be causing, some evil.

From this comes the tribal mask, that inscrutable gaze of the proverbial American Indian, that blank-faced, blind-eyed expression of a man in neutral, determined not to convey, emanate, anything. It's a flashlight turned off.

No one in a tribe can act, even exist, without affecting everyone else. Everyone affects everyone. So, much of the time, tribal man wears a stolid mask. He's like a beautiful woman who, to avoid advances, goes through life with downcast eyes. Unless he intends to, he isn't going to show emotion & thereby release a chain reaction that might shatter the togetherness of the tribe.

Humans are rarely depicted in Paleolithic cave art & when they are, they are almost always shown headless or masked, in relief. African masks generally show the eyes closed or slightly open; exceptions usually have fibres & fur scraps hanging over the eyes.

Egyptian figures were generally shown in relief, looking to one side. The Greeks liberated the human form from the back wall, but the facial expression remained empty: plantlike, slightly effeminate, the eyes unseeing. Yeats: ". . . their veiled glances." Roman art may have been lesser art, but the faces look back: their eyes engage our eyes. Literacy created a man who was no longer afraid to use his sight openly: to observe & be observed. The "unseeing tribal face" disappears with literacy.

It reappears with electricity: compare Praxiteles's youth with Paul Newman; Philas's athlete with James Dean or Marlon Brando: expressionless faces, half-closed eyes.

If there is such a thing as a "psychotic look"—and there are reputable psychiatrists who discuss this possibility—it's probably defined by absence of expression: not eyes glowing from an inner fire, but blank eyes, radiating nothing, no presence within. With the psychotic, this expression is largely, perhaps wholly, involuntary, in contrast to the "tribal face" of the young of today.

When the young talk among themselves, they tend to look off in different directions, rather than directly at one another. Girls wear dark glasses; boys affect the drooping lid: the eye is kept in neutral, two thirds closed, observing, missing nothing, but affecting nothing. Only when they're "turned on" do their eyes open wide: girls take off their dark glasses & emphasize eye makeup; boys raise their eyelids: then the eye transmits, gives out, reveals the inner self, and they lock in visual embrace, like Donne's lovers: "Our eye-beams twisted."

BREATH

Psychedelic artists speak of parallels between their visionary states & those reported in *The Tibetan Book of the Dead*. They sometimes sketch rays radiating out from chests or stomachs, in a manner reminiscent of Tibetan paintings. Contrary to what critics might predict, it's not sexual images most frequently dreamed of in such ecstatic states, but a form of breathing.

In the tribal world, the most powerful force radiating from any being is believed to be breath, which is regarded as life itself. God "breathed into his nostrils the breath of life, and man became a living soul."

In such societies, to speak means to call into being: "And God said, Let there be light; and there was light"; "By the word of the Lord were the Heavens made, and all the hosts of them by the breath of His mouth."

In Eskimo the word to make poetry is the word to breathe; both are derivatives of *anerca,* the soul, that which is eternal: the breath of life. A poem is words infused with breath or spirit. "Let me breathe of it," says the poet-maker & then begins: "I have put my words in order on the threshold of my tongue."

Swiss father:	*What is thinking really?*
Hilda (four	Don't know.
years, nine	*Well, what do you think with?*
months):	Animals think with their mouths.
	And people?
	With their tongues.
	What does a man do when he thinks?
	He speaks.

Children identify thinking "with the mouth" and thought with the voice. Thought is confused with the thing itself, in the sense that the word is part of the thing. Thoughts are word-things, stored in the breath or chest. The ears & mouth merely receive and transmit them.

Among the Trobrianders, *nanola* (intelligence, power of discrimination, capacity for learning magical formulae & nonmanual skills, as well as moral qualities) resides in the larynx. In locating it, Trobrianders point to the organs of speech. Memory (that store of formulae & traditions learned *by heart),* reside deeper, in the belly. Power is in words, not things: it resides within man & escapes through his voice.

Language is a storage system for the collective experience of the tribe. Every time a speaker plays back that language, he releases a whole charge of ancient perceptions & memories. This involves him in the reality of the whole tribe. Language is a kind of corporate dream: it involves every member of the tribe all of the time in a great echo chamber.

In *Beowulf,* "began to speak" is *unlocked his word-hoard* & *an opening word broke from his breast-hoard.* Society Islanders call thinking "speaking in the stomach" and thoughts "words in the belly." When a sacred recorder (harepo), famous in life for ancient knowledge, is dying, his son & successor places his mouth over the mouth of the dying man to inhale the departing soul; in this way lore is transmitted. Sages attribute their learning to this expedient.

When feelings & thoughts are regarded as work of the lungs, what could be more natural than the notion of "inspiration": inhaling the essence of another person or spirit?

Consciousness is naturally identified with breath: to be conscious is to have breath. The conception of words as part of the soul—the soul being that which survives death—may lie behind the poet's claim: Let no man mourn me.

What happens when a person—for the first time—sees himself in a mirror, in a photograph & film, hears his voice? The Biami of Papua cover their mouths. When a shy person in our society covers his mouth in embarrassment, we say he is "self-conscious." But why does consciousness of self produce *this* response? Does the anxiety of sudden self-awareness lead man to conceal his powers of speech-thought (his breath, his self) behind his hand, the way an awakened Adam concealed his sexual powers behind a fig leaf?

KEEP IN TOUCH

Cézanne: "Let us begin to paint as if we held things in our hands, not as if we were looking at them at all."

It was Impressionists who reminded us that the world contained "bodies": total, integrated. They allowed us to pick up that apple, see—smell—taste—swallow it. They broke with the noninvolved visual world.

With sight & hearing, we experience things *outside* of us; with taste & smell, only restricted parts of us are affected. But touch we feel *inside*: when we encounter an object, it resists, presses back, and thus we learn that the world is composed of other bodies. If it weren't for this, we would move through the world like phantoms. H. G. Wells tells a story of two-dimensional beings who can't enter our world of three-dimensional bodies. Two-dimensional beings can only witness the spectacle of life; they can't live in it. They see a criminal making ready to murder a sleeping woman, but they can't interfere, they can't warn her, and they suffer & are afflicted because their being is phantasmal.

TOUCH ME, TOUCH ME, LORD

In a literate, visual society, touch is avoided, while
in a tribal, nonvisual society, touch is a direct method
of receiving the essence of another. D. H. Lawrence in
The Blind Man tells how Maurice, who is blind,
attempts to communicate in words with Bertie, but
fails. Never having seen Bertie, he touches his face &
shoulders, then asks Bertie to do the same to him.
The emotions of the two men are diametrically opposed.
Maurice feels the "passion of friendship" & is
overjoyed: touch succeeds where words fail. But Bertie
is as Lawrence puts it, "annihilated" with fear that
by this intimacy he will be destroyed.

Visual, literate man avoided touch. But to tribal
man, touch is a direct method of receiving the essence
of another. Christ's miracles were performed by the
aid of His touch, although on one notable occasion the
healing was effected by a woman touching Him.

"I know my Lord laid His hands on me."

WHAT SURROUNDS, INVOLVES

We step into sound the way we step into a bath. We immerse ourselves totally. Religious conversion, or total acceptance, was symbolized by immersion in a river.

Today we immerse ourselves in sound. We've all become acoustic skindivers. Music is no longer for listening to, but for merging with.

"I can't talk about my singing; I'm inside it. How can you describe something you're inside of?" *Janis Joplin*

Girl: We were in the car one time and the wind was just banging in and the music was just banging out and you could hear it all around you. . . .

Boy: And I can get just completely involved in the music—just the music and me. . . .

Girl: It was just this bubble we were traveling along in—it wasn't like anybody else could hear, but— you know—we were just right inside everything;—and they've got the new sound—that kind of sound is the kind you can sandwich your head between two speakers and just take off. *Tony Schwartz recording*

The essential feature of sound is not its location, but that it *be.* Where the eye focuses, pinpoints, abstracts, locating each object in physical space, against a background, the ear accepts sound from all directions simultaneously. We say, "The night shall be filled with music," just as the air is filled with fragrance. We wrap ourselves in music.

Acoustic space is wrap-around resonance without fixed boundaries; Milton's ". . . dark / illimitable ocean, without bound / Without dimension. . . ." It contains nothing & is contained in nothing but, like the neo-platonist's definition of God, its center is everywhere, its boundaries nowhere.

"The room was humming harder / As the ceiling flew away." *Procol Harum*

Acoustic space is not pictorial, boxed in, framed; it's resonating, in flux, creating its own dimensions moment by moment.

I don't regard as accidental the close parallels between Eskimo art & Klee's & Miró's work. In each there is a structuring of space by all senses. Klee said his works owed more to Bach & Mozart than to any of the masters of art. He wanted art "to *sound* like a fairy tale," to be a world in which "things fall upward."

"Right now," said Miró, "I'm in a Bach mood. Tomorrow it could be Stockhausen. I'm very fond of the Beatles, too."

TASTE

Since the essence of a thing was thought to be its flavor, its aroma, to experience that essence directly meant taking it into oneself. One became what one ate.

The word "taste" itself originally had a much broader meaning than simply gastronomic experience. It meant *to explore, to test:* "Tasted the waye" (1480); "The men of armes entre into the dykes, and tasted the dykes with their speares, and passed over to the fote of the wall" (1525). It also meant *to have carnal knowledge of:* "You have tasted her in bed" *Cymbeline* II, IV (1611): "What, see, talk, touch, nay taste her!" (1752).

To be "out of taste" meant to be unable to distinguish flavors. "True taste" meant the sense of what is appropriate, harmonious, beautiful.

Children often explore by tasting. So do many natives. In Flaherty's *Nanook of the North,* Nanook examines a strange phonograph record by listening— seeing—touching—tasting. Lovers find each other "good enough to eat."

SMELL

The concept of an essence radiating out from an inner source applies to the other senses as well. Plutarch warned that not only fiery rays darting from the eyes, but the voice, breath & odor as well could harm, or aid.

Andaman Islanders paint themselves with clay to deny their odors to evil spirits.

Arabs consistently breathe on friends when they talk: "To smell one's friend is not only nice but desirable"; to deny him your breath is to deny him yourself.

Chuckchee of Siberia greet each other by sniffing down the back of the neck.

In the jungles of the Andamans, each flower period is thought to possess its own kind of force, of which the scent is the manifest sign and the fruit is the product. When a girl reaches puberty, she blossoms as it were, the later ripening being the birth of her children. Like the jungle plants, she is relieved to be under the influence of generative forces which everywhere produce blossoming & fruiting. She is therefore named after that particular odoriferous plant in flower when she reaches her blossoming time.

Certain remedies possess strong odors: Andamanese either eat them or breathe in their vapors: such odors, they say, effect cures.

This ancient belief has suddenly become very modern. The LSD trip is only a small part of it. It manifests itself in the most diverse ways. Young people burn incense; they smoke anything with a strong flavor. Men have become odor conscious; they aren't interested in *De*-odorants; they want powerful lotions, with earthy names like Lime, Peat, Brute. One kit contains four lotions, permitting you to mix your own depending upon the situation. Women smell men; they say, "You smell grand," or "I like that." A woman in love doesn't give a wallet; she gives a lotion. Lovemaking is no longer primarily visual. Sight has ceased to be the primary erotic sense: now it is touch, smell, taste.

SENSORY MIX

Common sense originally meant senses *communis*:
the power to translate each sense into the other,
without which no consciousness would be possible.

In the tribal world, the eye listens, the ear sees &
all the senses assist each other in concert, in a
many-layered symphony of the senses, a cinematic
flow which includes our "five & country senses."

. . . her vespers done,
Of all its wreathed pearls her hair she frees;
Unclasps her warmed jewels one by one;
Loosens her fragrant bodice; by degrees
Her rich attire creeps rustling to her knees. . . .
Keats

"He undressed me with his eyes" means he used
his eyes as all his senses.

"Listen to the green and feel it in your hands."
Tactility isn't just another sense: it has the power to
evoke or arouse the other senses. "He touched
me," begins a Negro spiritual, "and made me whole."

"Actually, his music is worse than it sounds."
Adults find a child's ability to learn a language
remarkable. But the child doesn't learn: he absorbs.

Language, to him, is a way of feeling, exploring,
thinking, fun. He becomes totally involved in the process
& is motivated by this total sensuous involvement.

"The more the arts develop," writes E. M. Forster,
"The more they depend on each other for definition. We
borrow from painting first and call it pattern. Later
we borrow from music and call it rhythm."

"The Voices restored: fraternal awakening of all
choral and orchestral energies and their instantaneous
application; the opportunity, the only one, for the
freeing of our senses."
Rimbaud

"I invented the color of the vowels!—*A* black,
E white, *I* red, *O* blue, *U* green—I regulated the form and
movement of each consonant, and, with instinctive
rhythms, I prided myself on inventing a poetic
language accessible some day to all the senses.
I reserve translation rights."
Rimbaud

Speaking of one person known to him, Eisenstein
said, "The scale of vowels was seen by him not as
colours, but as a scale of varying *light values.*"

All colors at once = white. "All the sounds of the
environment at once equal silence."
John Cage

VISUAL PUNS

Literate man can't see the rabbit & duck simultaneously.
Though he may switch rapidly from one to another,
he can't experience alternate readings at the same
time.

Tribal man can & enjoys doing so. An Eskimo
mask depicts walrus-wolf-seal; turned this way, walrus
is emphasized, but wolf-seal remain; turned another
way, wolf is emphasized, etc.

One may describe the alteration from duck to
rabbit as if the object had altered before one's eyes. But
what altered wasn't the picture, but the observer's
impression of it, his point of view, his emphasis upon
one organization over another.

Suppose he has no "point of view," at least none
resembling the private, delimiting one of literate man.
Suppose his art, language, everything in his culture,
deny a private point of view, and stress, instead, group
awareness, with many points of view sumultaneously
presented. Suppose, finally, he is capable of clasping
such a multi-level pattern instantaneously, with
total awareness, no delay, no suppression, all senses
simultaneously involved.

Suppose all this & you have gone a long way
toward describing tribal man, a man who has no private
point of view because he doesn't "view" experience,
nor conceive of himself as a "point." Instead, he
conceives of each person as participating in many
forces outside of himself & thus containing within
himself, simultaneously, many selves, all in flux.

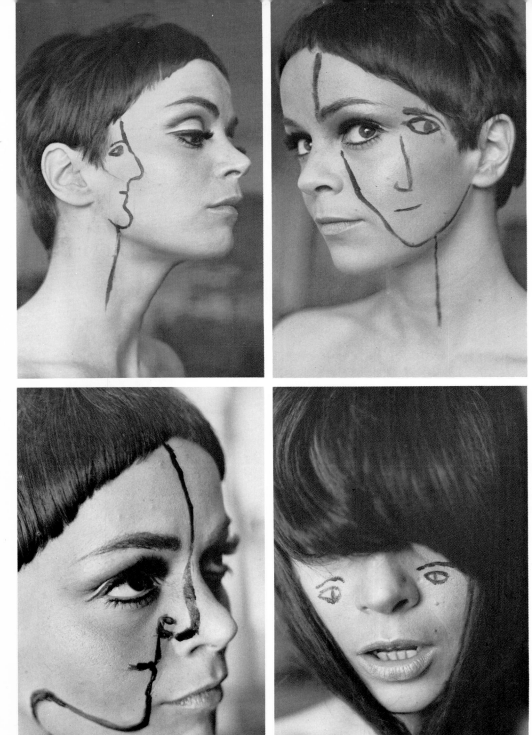

Sketches by Saul Steinberg

WHO DO I WANT TO BE TONIGHT?

"I wonder if I've been changed in the night?" asks Alice. "Let me think: was I the same when I got up this morning? I almost think I can remember feeling a little different. But if I'm not the same, the next question is, who in the world am I? Ah, *that's* the great puzzle!"

When Alice fell down that rabbit hole, she realized it was either very deep or she was falling very slowly, for she had plenty of time as she went down to look about her. Her adventures read like native myths, or modern physics, where each experience defines its own time & place.

" 'Who are *You*?' said the Caterpillar. . . . Alice replied rather shyly, 'I—I hardly know, sir, just at the present—at least I know who I *was* when I got up this morning, but I think I must have been changed several times since then.' "

At a court session in India, where a village woman was giving testimony, a judge told her, "Your testimony is false: last week you gave a different story." To which she replied: "This week I am a different person; if I had given you the same testimony, then I would have been false."

Literate man said: "A leopard cannot change his spots"; "One always knows just where he stands"; "We can count on his vote"; etc. But to tribal man, nothing, not even himself, remains the same for successive moments.

Where literate man regarded an alias as deceiving —*re*-presenting something other than the *real* self— tribal man often has several names, each a different facet of himself. He may also have several faces, each carefully painted, representing a different corporate self or role.

No one is deceived, nor meant to be. The mask wearer isn't *a* wolf nor *a* seal: he is Wolf, Seal: he participates *in* Wolf-ness, Seal-ness. These forms exist outside of him; they are public; but he can enter them & they can enter him, possess him: then he is Wolf, Seal.

In the tribal world, nothing has a definite, invariable shape. Like Echo, the mythical being who became all things, man is shape-shifting: by a sudden metamorphosis, he is this, now that. A Kwakuitl mask suddenly opens, revealing Bear; this springs apart— within is the face of another spirit. Such a mask expresses the variety & infinite subtlety of personality— its power of preserving due proportions between opposite elements—"and reveals undercurrents of desires & fears, long slumbering yet eternally familiar, which for thousands of years have lain near the root of our most intimate emotions & been wrought into the fabric of our most magical dreams."

THE MASK OF EVIL

On the wall hangs a Japanese carving
The mask of an evil demon, decorated with gold lacquer
Sympathetically I observe
The swollen vein of the forehead, indicating
What a strain it is to be evil.
Brecht

I CONTAIN MULTITUDES

The heroine of the play *The Beard* says, "Before you can pry any secrets from me, you must find the real me. Which one will you pursue?"

"Who am I?" In a world of electronic all-at-once-ness, everybody begins to include everybody else & many begin to feel the loss of their private identities. They feel deprived. Years ago, a man could say with pride & confidence: "I'm an American. A dentist. I have three children." This was his card of identity. Today such classifications aren't acceptable. Electricity abolishes the world of specialized human beings. The Western private "I"—aloof, dissociated—isn't possible when electricity involves us in the whole of mankind & forces us to incorporate the whole of mankind in us.

"Inner stability," so greatly admired by our grandparents, isn't possible when we're forced to shift our modes of perception abruptly. Stable experience is of little value when we face the Niagara of information made possible by electric technology. With the slightest shift in the sensory bias of a culture, the stable person is in real trouble. The fixed person for the fixed duties, once a necessity, is now a public menace. The specialist has become a comic figure, replaced by the artist.

Once the specialist, with his single set of skills, was seen as hero, while the whole man was seen as clown: the audience laughed at the clown's efforts to walk the tightrope. "Jack of all trades but master of none," was no compliment. But the tightrope walker & the flagpole sitter could each do but one thing: in a tribal or electronic society they could only be clowns. Today the generalist replaces the specialist.

The young no longer accept the traditional idea of a goal, of learning for a specialized operation or job. That vanishing point belongs to the past. Once you become an embalmer, you're dead. They prefer just finding out what's going on—the total field of operations. In a world where all paths seem to lead nowhere, distant goals become meaningless. "Where the action is" is "where it's *at*."

The young want roles, not goals. A role is a complex of unified activities. It's total. You step into it, participate in it. You can't participate in a job: you *work* at a job. A job is fragmented, specialized. It's not livable.

The young want many roles & they change behavior according to the role they are in & the clothes they wear. "I'm never sure," said Alice, "what I'm going to be, from one minute to another."

Sloppy, a character in Dickens' *Our Mutual Friend,* is described as a beautiful reader of a newspaper. "He do the Police in different voices."